UNKNOWN G
OF THE
SOUTH EAST

By Andrew Green

Edited by Trish Jones

*'Who is the third who walks always beside you?
When I count there are only you and I together
But when I look ahead up the white road
There is always another one walking beside you
Gliding wrapt in a brown mantle, hooded
But who is on the other side of you?'*

T. S. Eliot **The Waste Land**

S.B. Publications

By the same author:

Haunted Sussex Today	*Ghosts of Tunbridge Wells*
Haunted Kent Today	*Ghosts of the South East*
Haunted Houses	*Phantom Ladies*
Haunted Inns and Taverns	*The Ghostly Army*
Ghost Hunting: A Practical Guide	*Ghosts of Today*
Our Haunted Kingdom	*Which Witch*
Mysteries of Surrey	*Fancy Flights*
Mysteries of Sussex	
Mysteries of London	

First published in 2005 by S. B. Publications
Tel: 01323 893498
Email: sbpublications@tiscali.co.uk

ISBN 1-85770-313-8

Designed and Typeset by EH Graphics (01273) 515527
Printed by Ethos Productions Ltd.

Front Cover: Andrew Green photographed at Battle Abbey in the 1980s.

Back cover: Illustration from a postcard dated 1911 of a ghost at Hampton Court.

Acknowledgements

My sincere thanks go to the following people for their kind help and assistance in the compilation of this book:

John Andrews of Robertsbridge, David Bourne, Mrs Christian of Chertsey Museum, James Clark of Mitcham, John Dawes of Hawkhurst, Joan Dobson of Hastings, Roy Grant of Minster, Colin Harmer of Mountfield, Paul Harris of Folkestone, John Haynes of Winchelsea, Michael Jack of Hythe, Roger Jones of Mountfield, Jocelyn Kennard of Groombridge, Simon Kerr of East Grinstead, Quentin Letts of the *Daily Mail,* Alan and Jenny Marney of Battle, Lynn Merlin of Beckley, Alan Murdie, Valerie Nye of St. Leonards, Philip Paul of Guestling, Tom Perrott of The Ghost Club, Jack Pleasant of Peasmarsh, Malcolm Pratt of Bexhill, Ann Prince of St. Leonards, Brian Purdy of Hastings, John Rackham of Brighton, Sue Smith of Battle, Richard Sumner of Hastings, Nick and Margaret Taylor of Rye, Tunbridge Wells Borough Council, Yvonne Willis of Mountfield.

Special thanks are due to Kathy Gearing who provided valuable help with the Surrey cases; Philip Carr of Faversham for his considerable assistance throughout the whole compilation; Daryl Burchmore for the continued information regarding the Battle hauntings; Philip Hutchinson of Guildford for his fascinating material relating to his popular ghost walks of the city and surrounds: but really special appreciation is due to three ladies: - Trish Jones for so skilfully preparing the manuscript for production along with various useful comments, Lindsay Woods of S.B. Publications for her considerable patience and support, but above all my wife Norah Bridget for her constant encouragement and assistance throughout some difficult times.

Contents

Sussex

Introduction

The South East region of the United Kingdom not only consists of Kent, Surrey and Sussex but, as far as parts of the media are concerned, London as well. In a small selective work such as this it would be impossible to include the number of hauntings that affect the capital, but just to emphasise that ghosts are fully accepted "within government" Quentin Letts of the *Daily Mail* revealed, in an article on 20 November 2001, that the Pillared Room in 10 Downing Street is haunted by a woman in a long dress and pearls, known simply as the 'The Lady'. The *10 Downing Street Magazine* of 11 December 2001 pointed out that the room is currently used for official functions and the signing of international agreements.

"Witnesses to the haunting of 'The Lady' include several messengers and staff working in nearby offices, whilst police officers on duty and people in the garden have also reported ghostly footsteps being heard and a strong smell of cigars experienced in the basement rooms", but Churchill was not the only resident who smoked cigars there.

Author's drawing of the haunted Pillared Drawing Room at No. 10 Downing Street.

As more serious investigations are carried out into all aspects of the paranormal, and some results are featured in television programmes and publications of varying levels of authenticity and reliability, attitudes towards the acceptance of apparitions are, thankfully, changing. Dr Richard Wiseman's investigations at Hampton Court, in Surrey, provoked much debate about the use of his electronic response units in an attempt to obtain some scientific evidence of haunting. Tony Cornell of Cambridge, another highly respected researcher, however, has conflicting views about geomagnetic variations affecting human perceptivity and, raising yet another aspect, John Rackham, author of *Brighton Ghosts and Hove Hauntings* (Latimer Publications 2001) points out that since the 1920s modern ghosts are usually seen in coloured clothing, whilst those of earlier times appear mostly in monochrome. This, perhaps, strengthens an idea that I broached in the 1970s, that the process of witnessing is an electro-chemical one, in which the original image created was being 're-charged' through being seen. This effect re-establishes the initial appearance, but to confirm or 'set' the colours, it is necessary for the ghost to be seen fairly frequently, and if not, then the 'picture' or image reverts to grey, black and white or simply "a white shape". The extraction of heat from the locality at the time of the appearance, resulting in the witness feeling cold, confirms, I think, that an involuntary electro-chemical process is involved, and is nothing to do with fear. However the ghost at Greyfriars in Winchelsea produces a feeling of "great warmth" and conflicting completely with some thoughts is the claim that spectral Roman soldiers, seen for example in Dover, appear in their fully coloured uniforms. It is all rather intriguing and perhaps confusing, but enough of interest to ensure that the whole subject remains one of fascination to historians, archaeologists, scientists of varying disciplines, psychologists and of course to parapsychologists, but mainly to those who have encountered a ghost or two.

In April 2002 Sir Martin Rees stated in *Our Cosmic Habitat* (Weidenfeld & Nicholson), that he doesn't believe in alien visitation "any more than I believe in ghosts," as the evidence, he feels, is "flimsy". This may well refer to little creatures from Mars but there is sufficient evidence to convince High Court Judges, ancient philosophers, even politicians as well as a host of other scientists that phantoms are seen and have been experienced for centuries. *Fortean Times* declares that ufology is dead - but ghosts? - never!

Some witnesses have identified the phantom that they have seen which, for the strict rules of research, rather negates the value of the incident, for if they have observed someone they know to be dead, the sighting could so easily be self-deception, imagination, desire or even compassion. It is the case of the unknown figure that helps to heighten the argument for the existence of ghosts.

Perhaps they should be termed UMCI's - unintentional mind created images - for holograms and virtual reality pictures, although probably of the same actual width, are as tangible as each other, and have as much physicality.

Ghosts, whatever they may be, or seem to be, do exist as some form of visual phenomenon, albeit hallucinations and can never carry out any physical act or harm, despite what some media sensationalists claim.

Some of the cases in this small assembly relate to alleged phantoms of identifiable, not 'unknown' ghosts, but these are associated with earlier apparitions or of doubtful instances in which the identity is not fully established. Also included are examples of poltergeist incidents which are certainly not of ghostly origin, but arise from stress or trauma suffered by a living individual associated with the affected locality. This accounts for many 'haunted' pubs and shops which, like the Pillow Talk premises in Margate, sometimes employ young teenagers or adolescents suffering from the problems of adult life. Closed circuit television cameras could perhaps be used to illustrate the cause of the mysterious incidents but potential customers would probably be reluctant at being seen 'on camera'.

Criticism is sometimes levelled at reports regarding hauntings on sites which may be seen to profit from the publicity, ignoring the fact that the owners and proprietors of such premises also risk ridicule and loss of trade by revealing their problems.

All I hope is that you enjoy the following small collection of what I believe to be genuine cases, all experienced in the last 25 years, which could well add to the belief in at least some forms of the paranormal.

Andrew Green
Mountfield 2004

Bearsted

COBHAM MANOR RIDING CENTRE

In August 1985 Martin Emmott videoed his wife and their 10 year old daughter trotting round the riding circuit here, "really just to celebrate Janet's return to the saddle after 20 years absence", but it was only when they were watching the result the following afternoon, that they realised that there was something unusual about the incident. Just behind Kirsten, on her pony, there is "a ghostly Quaker-like figure" who "was certainly not there when I filmed", Martin said, and Janet confirmed, "that categorically, there was nothing unusual seen there at the time."

More information appears in *Haunted Kent Today* (1999), but since that was published further research details carried out by investigators have been revealed. Tony Cornell of Cambridge brought in a number of sophisticated electronic response units and

Martin Emmott's 1985 picture of his wife Janet and daughter Kirsten with the mysterious figure between them.

equipment in the hope of recording unusual factors affecting the area, but without success. However, a member of the Ghost Club, Natalie Osborne Thomason, a 'sensitive', was able to locate the precise spot where the phantom appeared on the video. She was surprised, as were many others, to be told later that on the other side of the hedge was the site of the 'lost' village of Aldington, once a thriving community until Black Death decimated the region.

In the 1990 reprint of the second 1949 edition of *Haunted England* by Christina Hole, there is a report of a ghostly horseman "sometimes seen in a lane which leads from the Pilgrim's Way to Bearsted and is often mistaken for a living person until he disappears where there is no gap or turning." This could well be the same location as that of the mysterious apparition that was recorded in 1985, and precisely the same area that the owner of the Riding Centre admitted was where some of his horses "have been spooked and seem to be quite agitated."

Bridge

HIGHAM PARK

There are not many country houses that can boast of having a list of visitors and former owners as noteworthy as this 14th century manor. Built originally in 1320, it has at one time catered for such personalities as Mozart and Field Marshal Montgomery, General de Gaulle and Thomas Culpeper, but of current interest is the fact that Ian Fleming, of '007', fame was a frequent visitor there for it was the home of his father Walter Whigham of the Bank of England.

Also among the distinguished owners was the Countess Zborowski (nee Astor) and her son Count Louis who created the famous 'Chitty Chitty Bang Bang' racing cars, one of which, a Grand Prix Mercedes, is reputed to be "buried 20 feet down somewhere on the estate". A photo of one of the huge vehicles parked in front of the building in the 1920s can be seen among other fascinating memorabilia displayed in the magnificent home, but the driver has not been identified.

The estate was finally purchased in 1995 with the intention of restoring what appeared to be a semi-derelict property, and in the course of achieving this the new owners have learnt of many fascinating aspects concerning its history that have never before been recorded.

I spoke to one of the proprietors, Amanda Harris-Deans in February 2003 to follow up my original entry relating to the haunting detailed in *Haunted Kent Today*, to ascertain if any new incident had been experienced. Amanda told me that a number of visitors had commented on the sound of a large car being driven up to the front door, but it remained invisible even when a short time later the scrunch of wheels is heard as the vehicle moves away. "I don't believe in ghosts," she assured me, "but I know that several people have experienced some unusual things here, the most puzzling is the appearance of a tall distinguished looking lady in a grey gown who has appeared in the walled garden that we have only recently been able to restore. Perhaps she is a relative of the Count

Higham Park, Bridge

or even maybe the Countess herself."

"We are in the course of opening up the top floor rooms and are fascinated by finding records of the occupation by the Army in the 1940-1950 period. It seems likely that even Winston Churchill paid a visit here, but I didn't know it was used as a hospital."

Joan Bell, a former nurse, had told me that when she worked there she had witnessed the figure of a strange man who vanished when she walked towards him to enquire what he wanted. "I learnt later that his appearance matched that of Perry Thomas, the Count's chief designer, who was killed in the crash on the Pendine Sands in 1929."

One of the results of the on-going renovation process was to arrange a sale of antiques in the autumn of 1998. It was at the end of this that one of the staff employed by Phillips, the auctioneers, turned back to enquire from Patricia Gibb as to the identity of the "unusual looking lady carrying a candle walking through one of the rooms on the top floor." The witness was assured that no-one could be there for "so far we have not unlocked any of those rooms. It is all sealed up and empty." It is in this area that intriguing documents and records are now being found, adding even more to the title of 'Higham, a house of a discovery'.

Canterbury

CANTERBURY CATHEDRAL

There are a number of ghosts that have been witnessed here over the years, which is hardly surprising considering the activity seen within its ancient walls. The first edifice was constructed in 597AD and used to baptise King Ethelbert, and the murder of Thomas Becket will never be forgotten thanks to the 'mediaeval painting' known as 'Becket's ghost' to be seen on a pillar in the crypt. It is however far more likely to be a representation of a saint, though because of its faded outline it is now difficult to assess exactly what it portrays.

Canterbury Cathedral's choir screen where the apparition of a woman in a long blue dress has been observed.

Joan Forman writes with emotion about Canterbury "if the living part of a human being - its energy or spirit - must remain on earth... perhaps no better environment could be found for it than this majestic building."

An excellent example of a crisis apparition was reported in *Haunted Churches* by Graham McEwan who detailed an incident involving the envoy of the Archbishop of Canterbury, Terry Waite. At the time, September 1987, he was being held hostage in the Lebanon. He is well over 6ft 6ins tall and is not easily mistaken, yet one evening a visitor from Manchester saw Terry, "quite clearly" standing silently with head bowed in front of the tomb of St Augustine, but as she watched the "phantasm of the living" slowly faded, leaving the witness "greatly moved and with belief that the sight was a sign of the speedy release of the popular cleric." He was able to return to his "beloved Canterbury" sometime later.

Rhona Martin, a well-known novelist best known for her prize winning work, *Gallows Wedding,* was so impressed with her experience seeing the hooded figure of a monk walking the cloisters here, that she became a researcher into the paranormal, especially "the world of ghosts," she told me.

More recently reports have been received regarding the figure of a woman in a "long blue dress" seen near the choir screen, but so far no information has been forthcoming as to her identity or any suggested reason for her appearance.

DOVER CASTLE

One of the most popular tourist attractions in the South East, is this 12th century castle, built originally to protect the country from invasion by marauding pirates and later Napoleon's army, but is best known these days for its 'secret' underground command centre used extensively during WWII and often visited by Winston Churchill, when Prime Minister.

Despite the view of Dr. Richard Wiseman there are a number of genuine ghosts which continue to be witnessed and, to my belief, recorded by way of a camcorder. Some details are given in the 1999 edition of *Haunted Kent Today* which describes the all-night vigil by a combined group of members from the Thanet Research Unit, ASSAP and individual expert investigators such as Dr. Chris Cherry from Kent University.

A male figure dressed in the style of a 17th century Cavalier has often been reported, as well as that of a woman wearing a red flowing dress. A pikeman was reported in 1979 and a man in a blue

An early 19th century engraving of Dover Castle.

cloak, but in 1991 an American couple were upset by the sound of screams and moans that they heard when in St. John's Tower. It is here that some of the inexplicable incidents occur with the sound of a large and heavy wooden door being slammed shut being the most noticeable and frequently experienced.

Part of the organised investigation was shown on Meridian television in a mini-documentary, in which a pair of massive wooden doors were seen to be shaken by some invisible force for several seconds, accompanied by Dr. Cherry's voice calling out "I think we've got that. It's incredible." At the same time a shadowy figure was seen moving silently up a nearby stairway.

Other sounds of the ghostly voices, similar to those of Churchill and Admiral Ramsey discussing the Dunkirk evacuation, have also been reported and, more recently, noises resembling those of the sobbing of a distressed woman, often associated with the witnessing of the figure of a "middle-aged woman in a darkish crinoline" in the same locality.

A somewhat puzzling incident was reported in the national press in May 2003 in which the four year-old son of Ian Stafford of Hucknall, Nottingham asked his father if he had seen the soldier. The description of the figure seen by the young boy matched that of the uniform of the 1940s. The site of this haunting was what had been an operating theatre, laid out "as if recently used, complete with bandages and surgical instruments" and to one side was a metal door that obviously had not been opened for many years. The boy had seen the "soldier come out through the sealed doorway, walk across the theatre and out through the main door."

What I found of great interest is that the adults saw nothing and like the youngster in Guildford Castle the boy was able to provide a full and accurate description. This somewhat confirms that humans up to the age of about 10 can more easily perceive 'ghosts' and, also, it seems that at least in these two incidents the sighting was limited to a young boy.

Farningham
LION HOTEL

It is not often when researching for book material that one receives an immediate and favourable response to a query about hauntings. Too often the owner of the property is rightly

The Lion Hotel, Farningham.

cautious or dismissive or, as on one occasion, too amused to give any understandable reply because of their hysterical laughter.

However, on contacting Arron Morrison, manager of the Lion, a former coaching Inn, in July 2003, I was assured that "definitely this building is haunted and I can vouch for the fact that at least 20 members of my staff have experienced the ghost here." I was a little surprised as well to hear a discussion with the bar manager, one of two resident staff, that he had witnessed phenomenon "only this morning, I was woken about 3 o'clock," he said, "by the sudden change of temperature in the room. It's always happening in Room 6, but we don't know why."

In 1996 the Surrey Paranormal Society investigated the case and were able to obtain details which implied that the cause of the haunting is "Alice", a former servant girl, who hanged herself there during the Napoleonic War, on learning of the death of her lover. There is, of course, no tangible evidence for this, but no frightening apparition is involved, just the quiet sound of a woman's voice, trying to persuade someone to "go to the window" and, occasionally, tugging on clothing to move a witness nearer the view towards the Dover Road. Even a cocker spaniel was intrigued by some invisible something, to sit watching the doorway repeatedly for no apparent reason over a number of days.

Folkestone

MARTELLO TOWER NO. 3

Having once been custodian of a Martello Tower (The Wish Tower no. 73 in Eastbourne), I was very interested to see that Paul Harris has discovered what seems to be a genuinely haunted reminder of Britain's defence system during the Napoleonic era in Folkestone.

When in the Wish Tower at Eastbourne one evening I was assured by an hysterical woman visitor that " as a medium I can see five men over in that corner fighting - ooh - it's horrible. One of the soldiers has just been killed, he's French, oh my God, there's another one." Her husband stood placidly beside her assessing my reaction which I'm afraid was hardly responsive.

It was five minutes to closing time, it was still pouring with rain and I was keen to get back home rather than discuss fictional incidents with imaginative individuals. However I waited for the performance to end before pointing out that the French never landed at Eastbourne and there had been only one death recorded in the Wish Tower, and that was of Harold Hubert who had died there from severe influenza and bronchitis when living in the tower as a tenant in the late 1800s. The couple departed dejected and I packed up.

However, Paul Harris makes the same sort of factual assessment before including reports in his books. This one, accompanied by a remarkable photo by H. W. Gill of "a boy with a ghost of a girl or boy standing next to him" looking up towards the entrance of the tower, is one such example. It was taken in 1926 after a storm caused some slight damage following which Mr. Gill, the Borough Council photographer, was instructed to record the extent of the damage. Folkestone Heritage Research Group, of whom Paul Harris is a member, took over the running of the tower for a while. On Harris's first day he climbed to the top of the tower to raise the flag and felt that eyes were watching him, his first customer of the day also remarked that they felt they were being watched at the top of the tower. The feeling of being watched seemed to decrease as time went by, possibly as Harris became a familiar figure there. Another member of the group said that they clearly saw the figure of a young boy sitting on the floor in front of him, but for only a few seconds before vanishing. Other reports have included the sound of marbles being rolled down steps, the sound of feet walking up the metal stairway and the sudden darkening in the doorway, when in fact there was no one there. Harris also says that occasionally, just out of the corner of his eye, he has seen what appears to be a white figure. Whilst he has been able to provide explanations for several of these phenomena, he says there is definitely a strange atmosphere about the place, a fact confirmed by Tamasin Jarret, Shepway District Council's Tourism and Events officer, when she had to be there alone some evenings to lock up the premises.

Martello Tower No. 3, Folkestone.

Groombridge

GROOMBRIDGE PLACE, near Tunbridge Wells

Heralded as one of the main visitor attractions of 2002, with its 'enchanted forest, magic, mystery and Dinosaur Valley' the Groombridge estate also contains a magnificent private manor house, surrounded by a moat dating back to the 1230s.

The first owner was William Russell who owned estates both in Ireland and Lancashire and with his wife founded a chantry, an endowment for a priest to say mass daily for some deceased person, but the site of the associated chapel has been lost. When he died in 1261, the lordship of the manor fell vacant and was taken up by Henry de Cobham, who fought under Edward I in the battles to conquer Wales. It was during this period that a charter established a weekly Thursday market and a three day Fair in May which continued up to the early part of the 20th century.

In 1604 the estate was sold to "its most illustrious owner, Sir Thomas Sackville" who was to become one of the really successful men of England. Since the 13th century the Sackvilles have owned land at Withyham, some three miles away, but due to their failure with gambling were forced to sell Groombridge in 1618 to a friend, John Packer, and it was his son, Philip, who in 1676 was responsible for rebuilding the old house, thought at the time to be in a 'ruinous condition'.

Financial problems, however, continued to affect the estate and as a result the house was left empty for twenty years from 1735, during which period a gang of smugglers had taken control of the village, basing their headquarters in the Crown Inn. There have been numerous claims that a secret tunnel exists between the cellars of the Crown Inn and those of Groombridge Place but so far no trace of it has been discovered.

In 1754 the manor was saved from Chancery by William Camfield who carried out more restoration work and developed the long neglected gardens "at great expense". When he died in 1781 Robert Burges of Hall Place, Leigh, bought it and his widow remarried having let the property to her sister and brother-in-law, Elizabeth and John Saint, eventually allowing the Revd. John James Saint to live there as a real Victorian country squire, acting as both employer and charitable benefactor. Tenants were given Christmas dinners and coal on which to cook them, newborn babies were presented with a set of new clothes and a regular tea party was held in the grounds for the benefit of the villagers.

When the railway was built, with a tollgate, the Reverend Saint built himself a road to the station to save himself 'a penny a journey'. It remains still, but only as a footpath. He also fathered a son and three daughters. The boy, John James Heath, became a Catholic and on being promptly disinherited by his parents, emigrated with his family in 1880 to Australia. Sophia, the eldest daughter, became a lady-in-waiting to Queen Victoria and eventually moved to The Cottage on the estate with her naval officer husband and a large collection of canaries, much to the delight of the village children. She died in 1901 leaving her sisters Louise and Elizabeth to maintain the charitable traditions laid down by her parents.

Groombridge Place.

Visits from notable people include that of Sir Arthur Conan Doyle, who used Groombridge Place as the setting of 'Birlstone Manor' in his novel *The Valley of Fear*, published in 1915. But he also originated one of the estate's persistent ghost stories. In his well-known non-fiction work *At the edge of the Unknown* he tells of leaving the house one afternoon with an American psychic and "seeing a ghost standing in a cottage doorway which opens on to the moat". The figure, wearing a rust-coloured smock was witnessed soon afterwards walking a few paces behind the couple. It was Conan Doyle who established the identity of the phantom, being that of Dave Fletcher, who had been ostler at the Place and who lived in Moat Cottage with his mother until drowning in 1808. The apparition, however, has been seen since on a number of occasions, the most recent being in 1995.

Another incident that brought Groombridge to the attention of the general public was when it was used as the main set for the film *The Draughtsman's Contract* which in itself achieved cult status. The owner at the time, Stanford Walton Mountain died in 1984 aged 91, leaving the Place to his niece, Rosemary Newton, as the tenant for life, but she died quite suddenly only seven years later. The new owner, Andrew de Candole, sold the estate in 2001 but ensured that the gardens were made available to the public, and Groombridge Place itself remains as a private home.

It was the general manager, Jocelyn Kennard, who told me about the Moat Cottage ghost, but the appearance of David Fletcher is also mentioned in the *History of Groombridge* by Barbara Maidment. I was pleased to learn though that an apparition of an unknown lady in grey, wearing Victorian style riding jacket, was seen by a visitor in the morning room of the main house. Jocelyn also assured me that the smell of cigar smoke and the strong perfume of lavender has often been experienced at the bottom of the main stairway, but no one has yet identified the culprit, or the mysterious grey lady.

Hythe

SALTWOOD CASTLE

An 18th century engraving of Saltwood Castle.

Reputed to be one of the finest Norman Castles in private ownership, with a popular Battlement Walk round the Inner Bailey, Saltwood also houses a grim dungeon where 'Thorpe Lollard' was imprisoned for over 15 years. But Jane Clark, widow of the well-known 'character' and former Defence Minister, Alan Clark, assured me that it is the ghost of a monk that now visits one of the bedrooms of her home, and who has been witnessed there not only by herself, "more than once," but by a number of her friends and some guests. "There is nothing frightening about him," she said, "he is obviously a bit old and frail and all he does is to walk through the room where he vanishes at a blocked up doorway in one of the walls."

Another 'unknown' figure is that of a woman wearing a grey gown seen occasionally in the library "in the afternoons" by several visitors.

In the time of Henry II the castle was home to Sir Ranulf de Broc, sworn enemy of Thomas Becket. It was from here with an escort of Sir Ranulf's men that the four knights who were to end Becket's life set out in December 1170, and to Saltwood Castle that they returned after the grisly deed was done.

Shortly before he died in 2002, Alan confirmed his feelings that "someone" is buried in front of the steps of the 14th century gatehouse, "but there is no sense in digging up some old bones. Let the dead rest in peace."

Saltwood Castle in the 1920s.

Margate

Pillow Talk, Margate.

PILLOW TALK

One of the main causes of poltergeist phenomena, in which objects are apparently thrown around by their own volition, is sexual frustration, suffered mainly by adolescents, though others, at times, have similar problems. Moving house, divorce, menopause and bankruptcy are all concerns listed in the schedule of possible causes for the mysterious disturbances. Many newly-opened shops have been affected, for a short time, except those, like pubs, which have a constantly changing staff of youngsters.

No. 13 Marine Drive, a number which in itself may be a catalyst, Pillow Talk deals mainly with ladies underwear and sexy clothing and it seems is the centre for a fairly regular 'attack' by 'an unknown poltergeist'. Who exactly is responsible will probably be never known, despite the constant chaos being suffered "practically every day", according to Cilla George, the director of the business. She told me in July 2002 that she opens up at about eight in the morning, to find bras, knickers, thongs and other associated attractions scattered throughout the display and sales areas, despite having left the shop the previous night "all shipshape and Bristol fashion."

She also told me that the staff of four includes two younger members which, as with most retail premises in popular seaside resorts, constantly change. The associated shop next door, no. 12, which offers more specific aids for adult satisfaction, is rather surprisingly not affected, though both properties have been established for some 22 years.

Cilla has been working in Pillow Talk for about 10 years and like the owner, Mr Butler, is puzzled and more than a little irritated by the attention of the knicker twister. "One day," she said, with a grin, "we'll catch 'em. Then watch out!"

Minster, Isle of Thanet

OLD OAK COTTAGE

Thought to be the original guesthouse used to accommodate visitors and pilgrims to the nearby Minster Abbey in olden days, this private home, which was until about ten years ago a popular restaurant, was "most certainly up to several years ago haunted by poltergeist incidents." Roy Grant, custodian of the Minster Museum, told me that often the owners, having laid up tables for the following morning's breakfast, on opening up, would find all the cutlery and napkins moved around and sometimes "completely missing".

Prior to this, the ghost of an unknown monk, was "frequently seen" normally in September, for some mysterious reason, and then "as a shadowy outline against a bright light". His appearances were always heralded by the sound of shuffling sandled feet in one of the 'older' bedrooms. He was thought to be the brother appointed to act as host to the guests of the Abbey. Sir Arthur

Old Oak Cottage, Minster.

Conan Doyle is known to have stayed here for several nights to investigate hauntings, possibly of this monk.

A few years ago, when renovating this ancient building, the core of which is probably of 12th century construction, and excavating the cellars, remains of a tunnel leading to the Abbey were discovered. The Abbey itself was built in 950 AD and when religious conflicts became rife it is "highly likely that some people would use the tunnel to reach the hoped-for sanctuary."

In 2004 the house once again changed hands and once more alterations and renovations were undertaken. Late that year the present owner, John Walford, was called to see the drying plaster in one of the front bedrooms in which the image of a human skull, the height of the wall, was clearly visible. Still more remarkable was the fact that the plasterer had twice previously removed the plaster as the image was forming, to ensure his plaster mix was not contaminated. When the third and final image of the skull appeared in the drying plaster, although more or less the same as had appeared before, it was now about a third larger and clearly witnessed by five people in the room.

Even before the house was a restaurant, inexplicable sounds of "dragging footsteps" were reported, but as to who was involved remains a mystery.

Northfleet

YE OLDE LEATHER BOTTEL

In 1976, shortly after Mr & Mrs Mason took over ownership of this delightful old tavern, as rather expected, poltergeist activity started. Small plastic objects like ashtrays and coasters would disappear only to be found later "having moved by themselves to some most unlikely places."

About a year later, whilst chatting to three friends and a couple of the staff when the last customer had gone and the doors were all locked one evening, Janet saw the figure of a woman with dark brown hair "in a page boy fringe" move rapidly towards the bar. "She was wearing a greyish-blue fitted sleeve cardigan, and we just thought she was a customer accidentally locked in," she told me, "but she just vanished on reaching the counter."

A few weeks later, another ghost made its appearance. A young man with long fair hair was seen by a regular customer to walk

Ye Olde Leather Bottel Inn at Northfleet.

towards the wall of the kitchen and when only a couple of feet away from it, "just faded away." That haunting was experienced on at least three occasions during the following few weeks, both by staff and customers, all of whom were justifiably puzzled by the identity of the visitor. Due to the modern style of clothing worn and "their general appearance and bearing" the idea that they could well be phantoms of living people strongly connected with the pub was seriously considered, recalling the case of 'the crisis apparition of Terry Waite having been witnessed in Canterbury Cathedral in September 1987 (see *Haunted Churches* by Graham McEwan) when in fact he was being held prisoner in the Lebanon.

However, in April 2003, the current licensee, Gloria Plumb, confirmed that the more traditional type of ghost now seemed to reside in the inn, though of course, the poltergeist problem of "glasses flying off their hooks and on one occasion a basket of flowers fell off a six inch nail on the wall, but when I put it back, it just flew off again, straight away," still appears to exist.

Kathy Gearing of the Ghost Club, who kindly provided additional material following an investigation of the haunting, told me that Gloria had also reported the appearance of a "ghostly man in a black cloak" who, it was thought, was a phantom of a suicide many years ago. "What I cannot understand," Gloria admitted, "is that things seem to happen when I'm not there. But it doesn't worry me at all now, even though it is now really obvious that we have a ghost here."

The building was originally three farm cottages facing across the Dover Road over the Thames to Tilbury, and may have been at one time linked to the popular smuggling that was rife in the area. With a laugh, the landlady issued a challenge, "if you don't believe in ghosts, pay us a visit!"

Otford

OTFORD ANTIQUES AND COLLECTORS' CENTRE

A small group of members of the Ghost Club visited this intriguing old building in 2001, following a report in a local paper that it was haunted, but not surprisingly they were a little disappointed at experiencing nothing unusual during their investigations.

I spoke to the owner, David Lowrie, in August 2002 and he admitted that whatever it was that had created interest from the local paper and the Ghost Club, "seems now to have died down, or died away. We thought it might have been the ghost of Bill Hope, the manager of the

Otford Antiques and Collectors' Centre.

original hardware store here. He was also the caretaker of the Village hall, but died in 1980 when he was 80 years old." The reason for the possible identification was that the figure seen seemed to be similar to that of 'Old Bill'. "It was of a man with short greyish hair and wearing the sort of coat Bill had," Elaine told him, "and there was a strong smell of pipe tobacco wafting around." The ghost had been witnessed a few times, in the evenings walking through the shop going towards the stairway, by one or two customers and members of the staff, but was always surrounded by a cloud of smoke.

The main area of 'the haunt' was at the top of the stairs, which in the previous occupation had been a hardware shop, where Old Bill, or Popeye as he was also known, would be working. Some of the staff of the 30 dealers that now occupy the premises are still reluctant to work near there. "Perhaps it's because of the smell of the pipe."

Mr Hope had been a constant pipe smoker, and despite the noticeable request for 'No Smoking' in what would now be a fire risk area, the odour of pipe smoke still pervades the building, but only on occasions.

But the main problem these days is the mystifying disappearance of some of the main antique items, David told me. "A couple of weeks ago two young customers asked me to keep a couple of special items for them, as they planned on giving them as gifts to members of the family. I put them, as usual, in a special locker beside the counter where I work, but when the customers arrived a few days later the items had vanished. It was more than a little embarrassing. But this sort of thing keeps on happening. It can't all be small pilfering or forgetfulness as my wife confirms. We reckon it could be Bill, but of course it might well be something else. I just wish they would stop smoking though. It really is getting annoying."

Westerham Hill

HAWLEY'S CORNER

In January 1997 a witness to a mystifying incident experienced what may be connected with a horrifying air crash. She was collecting her two sons from the Spinning Wheel Restaurant where they worked, but as she drove towards the building she saw in the headlights of her car the figure of a young man "with very blond hair, wearing a leather flying jacket and carrying a helmet." Neither of her sons saw the 'pilot' but on making enquiries from one of the officers of the Air Training Corps at nearby Biggin Hill airfield they were told that a Hawker Hurricane fighter aircraft had crashed "on that corner some years ago."

What seems confirmatory evidence was a report from a London Transport official carrying out a passenger survey in the same locality some four years later. The driver of the bus allocated to the task asked the operative whether he believed in ghosts, and although receiving a negative answer insisted on telling him of his experiences.

"I was doing a similar run like today and approaching Biggin Hill when I distinctly saw the figure of a man waiting at the aerodrome bus stop at Hawley's Corner. As I got nearer I could see that the chap was wearing the uniform of the 1940s and thought I must be imagining things, but just as I reached the stop the figure just vanished. I heard later that there had been the crash of a fighter plane there but no one seemed to know when. Perhaps it was even during a flying display at Biggin Hill."

Surrey

Chertsey

GEORGE INN

Thought to be the oldest pub in the town, having been built in the 13th century as a hunting lodge for King John, this ancient structure took its name after a visit from George III, but it also claims fame for being referred to by Charles Dickens in his *Oliver Twist*.

A former colleague of mine, Jack Hallam, was one of the first to reveal that the pub contained a ghost in his excellent book *Haunted Inns of England* 1970, but sporadic weird incidents are still experienced according to the current owners, Kelly Geddes and Jonathan Whiting.

In the 1960s a married couple staying there had noticed that their bed had suddenly sunk down in the middle as if someone had thrown a heavy weight on it, or a very large person had "just flopped down for a rest."

The bar manager, Paddy, told me in July 2003 that he had heard footsteps walking across an empty room on a couple of occasions and was still trying to find an explanation for other peculiar incidents such as glasses moving about and the weird atmosphere that suddenly and inexplicably affects one of the bedrooms. "Oh, yes," he said, "The George is definitely haunted. We reckon the ghost is that of a monk who killed himself because of committing some ghastly sin. We call him Mr. Heavy."

George Inn, Chertsey

Dorking

POLESDEN LACEY

Stated to have been erected in 1632 as a villa for the Castleton family, the building was considerably altered during the Edwardian era for the subsequent owners. In 1747 trustees of William Moore had

An early 19th century scene at Polesden Lacey.

sold Polesden Lacey to Francis Geary, later to become a baron.

His son enlarged the estate and sold it to Richard Brinsley Sheridan, the famous dramatist and author of *The School for Scandal*, but on his death in 1816 the property became deserted and the grounds neglected.

Thankfully, though, it was saved when Charles Sheridan sold it to Joseph Bonsor who restored and improved it, mainly by rebuilding the present house on exactly the same spot as the original and using much of the former's materials.

By 1939 Mrs. Greville, a well-known hostess, had become the owner and had entertained many distinguished guests here, including George VI, when Duke of Kent, for part of his honeymoon.

On the death of her father in 1942, and as a memorial to him, Mrs Greville left the property to the National Trust which has been responsible for it and the estate ever since.

The National Trust representative claims that "the house is certainly not haunted." However in one of the 'great gardens', there is a small wooden bridge and it is in this immediate area that an apparition has been witnessed on a number of occasions. "It is dressed in long brown robes with a hood pulled down so low that no part of the face can be seen," reported one of the visitors. Also "a strange whistling sound has been heard near the Nun's Walk," but there is probably a rational explanation for this, though none has been offered so far.

 Farnham

THE CHURCH OF ST. ANDREW

This charming old building, to be found behind West Street, has long been haunted by the sound of a High Mass being celebrated, with the strong smell of incense together with the chanting that accompanies the service.

The visual appearance of the ritual has also been reported on a number of occasions during the last few years and one visitor was able to describe members of the ghostly congregation as well as the celebrant and his assistants, before the whole vision dispersed on the arrival of the churchwarden.

A more distressing incident has been the sight of an old lady in white who, after entering the church, is next seen at the top of the tower where she leaps from the parapet only to vanish before reaching the ground.

PIZZA PIAZZA RESTAURANT

When he was a student in 1948 at the Castle Theatre, Edward Woodward, later to become famous as a TV actor, described an experience there that he has never forgotten. The building in Castle Street had been an old barn and earlier a bakery, but now it is a popular restaurant though still affected, it seems, by 'the paranormal'.

Pizza Piazza, Farnham.

Woodward witnessed not a 'ghostly figure', but a really weird incident in which the curtains in the dormitory, which he shared with several members of the cast of a forthcoming production in a Weekly Rep performance, were seen to be "all standing out into the room", as if on wires. All the windows were wide open and even though the evening had been very hot the room was "amazingly cold, like ice", and there was no sound, just silence. The actor rushed downstairs, calling out for his colleagues to come and look, and yet when they reached the dormitory the curtains had returned to their normal position and every window was not just shut, but locked.

The lady who ran the theatre, Joyce Buckle, associated the incident with the recent death of her husband, but others recalled the suicide of an old baker who had hanged himself in the main hall, though more recently, Jean Parratt told me, the figure of an unidentified actor has been seen on a number of occasions. Called 'Rotca' - the reverse of 'actor' - by some, he was witnessed walking along a corridor on the top of the stairway, during the summer of 2002 by some members of the restaurant. But another well-known personality, Sir Michael Redgrave, also referred to the haunting. "Whenever I played there, I really felt the presence of the phantom," he told the staff.

Laura, the supervisor of the Pizza Piazza, said that she had never experienced anything unusual there, but quite believed others had seen the mysterious figure.

Guildford

ANGEL HOTEL

With a history going back to the 14th century, it is not really surprising to learn of stories of ghostly incidents affecting this popular hotel in the main High Street. The most publicised case, a few years ago, was the apparent haunting by a soldier in the uniform of the Polish Army of "about the 19th century", seen only in the mirror on a wardrobe door in room No. 1, known as the Prince Imperial of France Room. The image was so clear to the witness that they were able to make a fairly accurate sketch of it which was published in *The Haunted Inns of England* by the late Jack Hallam.

Since then alterations and modernisation seem to have exorcised the soldier for he has not been seen for some time. However, as recently as September 2002, according to the hotel's receptionist

Angel Hotel, Guildford.

The drawing made by the witness of the Polish soldier seen at Guildford's Angel Hotel.

and deputy manager, the figure of an unknown man has been seen walking through the closed door of one of the bedrooms, stop and glance out of the window to return and fade back through the door. One witness, Pamela Chandler, told me that she saw the spectral shape when staying in the hotel, "years ago" and a member of staff had also reported to Stuart Warren, the deputy manager, that he too had witnessed the same figure when approaching the room one evening. He also saw one of the bedroom chairs move "about six inches of its own accord towards the window - it was really weird."

I was also assured that "pots and pans and a number of small items of kitchen equipment have often been seen to move around by themselves" in the breakfast room, which now forms part of the 13th century crypt.

The staff there are also "quite used to the sound of unattached footsteps" that they hear walking through the restaurant. A mysterious male figure, "and no, it's not the chef", has also been observed gliding through the room "sometimes in the evening. But we are not worried by it. Why should we be?"

CLOTH HALL - EDINBURGH WOOLLEN MILL

According to Philip Hutchinson, former custodian of Guildford Museum, this building was constructed by George Abbott, Archbishop of Canterbury, in 1619 and was initially linked with Waverly Abbey near Farnham through its religious associations, but was to become a hospital and eventually this retail outlet, having changed hands on a number of occasions. It was recently a Laura Ashley shop, an appropriate use for Cloth Hall as it was, for some time, the centre of Guildford's Blue wool trade.

During the conversion period in the 1990s, when Mike Davies was in charge of the work force, the sound of a girl crying was frequently heard, as well as the unusual sound of a trumpet being played, "over four or five days". Mike was so mystified that contact with a 'psychic' was arranged in an attempt to clarify the mystery.

Cloth Hall, Guildford.

On examining the property and the exact site from which the sounds originated, the 'medium' claimed that when the building was used during the Victorian era as a boys' school, two girl pupils had been so badly beaten that one died in the room on the upper floor, but what the connection was with the sound of the trumpet remains a mystery, as does the fact that the school was supposed to deal only with boys.

Whilst the workmen

were carrying out the extensive renovation it was noticed that in the room from which the crying had been heard the windows would often be found in the mornings to be wide open, though obviously for security and safety reasons they had been closed and locked the previous night.

Some years earlier, in 1979, two members of the staff at the time, Julia and Sarah, were surprised and startled to hear, when working in the stock room on the top floor, three loud and very distinctive raps at the window and, looking towards it, saw a vague misty shape clouding and obliterating the glass. Unable to find an explanation, and slightly disturbed, they were even more apprehensive when reaching the stairway outside, having locked the door of the room, to hear the sound of conversation coming from the empty store room. "Although clearly people were talking, the words were muffled and we were unable to distinguish what was being said," Julia said later.

Currently the atmosphere in the 'stock area' remains a "bit mysterious".

GUILDFORD CASTLE

The castle itself was constructed between 1066 and 1071 by William the Conqueror, and remained a royal residence, or at least a royal property up to the reign of Henry III. All that is left now is the Norman keep containing the original dungeons from which in 1391 a number of prisoners escaped.

The most unusual haunting here occurs "usually about once a year, in the autumn", but always when a young woman with a son of "about 3 years of age, some though have been 6 years old", visits the site. Custodians over the years have repeatedly recorded that a young mother with a little boy "crying his eyes out and obviously very distressed" has reported that, each time, the lad has been very upset to "see a man chained to the wall in the dungeon and wants to know why they were not warned about the dummy figure." It is only when the mother is taken back to reassure her that there is no such figure in the ruin that she accepts that, together with a number of other mystified visitors, her son has witnessed an apparition of the past.

It is perhaps of interest to recall the study of child perceptivity carried out by the author in the 1950s and enlarged by Dr. Ernesto Spinelli of Surrey University, which indicated that human 'awareness' and what some may term as 'psychic sensitivity' peaks at about seven years of age. Some American 'ghost hunters', I am led to believe, used children of "about 7 years of age, together with genuine clairvoyants and the occasional dog" to act as "detectors" before sophisticated instrumentation was designed to register changes in atmosphere, electro-magnetic variations and other such aspects that might account for examples of the paranormal. Why only boys seem to be 'receivers' at Guildford adds to the mystery.

Guildford Castle.

GUILDFORD MUSEUM

Owned and administered by the Surrey Archaeological Society is this fascinating museum conveniently sited opposite one of the reasons for visitors to the City, the ancient castle, but which also contains items connected with Lewis Carroll, the author of *Alice in Wonderland,* who died in Guildford in 1898.

Guildford Museum.

Original parts of the museum date from 1256 but additions effected between 1630 and the 20th century complete the structure as it can be seen today and it is here that one of the unknown ghosts of the County resides.

Quite recently a few local residents and members of the staff have heard the sound of someone playing the piano coming from one of the empty rooms on the upper floor. Peter Sager, a resident caretaker, reported that he had often tried to trace the actual source of the noise but is totally unable to explain it.

Whether there is any connection with an incident experienced by another staff member is still debated upon. He was about to start checking literature stocks retained in the cellar but was a "little upset" on reaching the bottom of the stairs to see "a cloud of what looked like flour form itself into the shape of a young woman which then moved quite quickly to a nearby wall and melted into it." It is thought to be where there was once a staircase leading to the upper floors, but whether this apparition was that of the phantom piano player or not will probably never be known.

THE KING'S HEAD

Although the building itself was constructed in the early 1600s, the pub here moved from a nearby site because of its popularity bringing so much increased trade that the older house a few yards away couldn't deal with it. But even with such a change, and its once rowdy reputation, no weird incidents took place until 1987 when the head barman one night was suddenly horrified to see "the ghost of an old lady, grey and indistinct", standing beneath one of the old beams. Adding to his distress was the fact that only he could see the phantom.

This was followed by the pub dog "going mad", and having calmed down, barking somewhat savagely at the spot in the wall where a blocked up doorway used to lead to the cellar. It is here that some staff members have also heard a woman's voice calling out to them to go downstairs, only for them to find the area deserted.

In his report to the Ghost Club, Philip Hutchinson tells of the bar ceiling suddenly caving in during February 1995, due to the activities of the dreaded Death Watch beetle. During the resultant restoration evidence was discovered by archaeologists of a mediaeval building on the site which suggested it was a cobbler's shop.

But this seems unconnected with the current haunting during which the figure of a small girl in a white Victorian dress has been seen by at least a couple of members of the staff, "standing by the entrance before skipping through the bar and disappearing through the French windows into the beer garden." In addition to this unidentified spectre, the ghost of a man has also been witnessed sitting at a table by a front window.

122 HIGH STREET (JIGSAW)

In 1953, in order to complete the conversion of the Corona coffee shop on this 13th century site on time, the work force brought from London agreed to stay actually on the premises for a couple of nights, having already equipped themselves with sleeping bags and camping equipment. On the first night, though, they were woken in the early hours by the sound of a female voice coming from a room immediately above their sleeping quarters, despite the fact that it had been blocked up for decades. The talking was as if the woman was holding a conversation with someone she disliked, but the actual words were so muffled as to be unintelligible.

When the talking stopped heavy slow footsteps were heard walking round the closed, empty room and clearly the sound of rustling skirts or dresses, and then to add to the distress of the men below, the sound of someone coming down a staircase that they had removed the previous morning. On reaching the floor the footsteps resumed until just fading away on reaching one of the outer walls. So intrigued were the group that they called on the Ealing Psychical Research Society to investigate, but they discovered nothing to account for the haunting. However, when a wall in their temporary quarters was demolished a previously unknown room was revealed, containing a complete Tudor fireplace and window, and whilst knocking down another part of the wall a second window was discovered in one of the cavities, together with the skeletons of eight cats.

122 High Street, Guildford where footsteps were heard to descend a staircase which had just been removed.

During the demolition process of the nearby Baptist Chapel in 1954 the figure of a lady in a long grey dress had been reported by the workmen, seen walking sedately and silently through the dust and rubble before disappearing on her way, it seems, to Tuns Gate.

In 1985 three girl students were renting a room on the first floor of the same building when, one night in July, they all heard heavy limping footsteps, accompanied by the sound of a crinoline skirt rustling through the area. They waited, with some apprehension, for something, anything, to happen and within a few minutes saw a dim blue shimmering light appearing at the top of the adjoining staircase. The light eventually became "as strong as a torch beam, until suddenly it switched off". The girls were so upset by their experience that they were able to persuade a local priest to bless the place.

But when the clothing shop was opened some years later two members of the staff were astonished to see the same "sedate lady in a long grey dress" walking up the main stairway. When one of the girls tried to locate the mystery customer she was told, "Don't bother. You have just seen the ghost. She doesn't trouble anybody, but no one knows who she is, though she has been seen a number of times. She is just a shade from the past."

WATERSTONE'S BOOK SHOP

One night in 1995. when this High Street shop was 'Principles Men's Wear', the appointed key holder was annoyed to be woken by the local Police who had found all the alarm bells ringing, "disturbing the residents".

On entering the premises, the manager found a WPC sitting on the stairs with his young four year-old son. She had taken charge whilst his father was dealing with the outside alarm system, and the two had been playfully chatting and sorting through a number of stickers that the boy had been given "by Daddy". Suddenly, though, the youngster turned and looked behind the woman and started talking quite earnestly to someone that she couldn't see. "It's a nice old man, standing there behind you," said the boy, "he's got a funny little black hat on." It was soon discovered that the fault of the bells had been caused by an electrical malfunction, and the Police departed leaving the manager to stack the stickers carefully on the corner edge of one of the stair treads, before locking up and returning home.

On arriving at the shop the following morning he was astounded to find that all the stickers had been peeled from their backing cards and placed in a perfect circle on one of the windows. Later he was told, but is not convinced, that this was a former symbolic Jewish rite.

Earlier that year, 1995, when the building was being prepared for the new owners, a 12th century Jewish Scroll Reading room had been discovered beneath the foundations of the shop premises. It was during that period, the 1100s, that it was illegal to practice openly one's Jewish faith and the suggestion is that the room, rather like a Priest's Hole, was used as a secret room for worship.

The source of this report, Philip Hutchinson, events' officer of the Ghost Club and organiser of the highly popular Ghost Walks of Guildford, told me that he had discovered, when custodian of the Guildford Museum, a man named Isaac, the treasurer of the nearby Castle, had once lived in a building on the High Street and suggested that the figure seen by the youngster was that of the treasurer, but of course it might not have been.

Hampton

HAMPTON COURT PALACE

Claimed rightly by Joan Foreman in her brilliant book *Haunted Royal Homes* to be the loveliest palace on the banks of the River Thames, this once centre of regal activity, built by Thomas Wolsey, a butcher's son later to be England's prominent Cardinal, must also be one of the most haunted royal establishments in the country housing, it is claimed, some 25 apparitions. Unfortunately for this small collection practically all the ghosts and phantoms that have been witnessed have been identified, few are unknown and even fewer witnessed in the last couple of decades.

However, in 1995, John Chalcroft, a steward stoking up fires in the Tudor kitchen, "near the monk's ancient burial ground" suddenly glanced through the archway leading to another part of the kitchen, and from a wall "came a misty grey disc about 18 inches in diameter." The weird shape drifted across the kitchen and disappeared but two days later, at about the same time, eleven in the morning, the incident repeated, and John also learnt from a colleague that they had witnessed the same peculiar object, "and no, it wasn't a flying saucer", but shaped like an old wooden platter.

A more traditional haunting of a figure is that which visits an apartment in Fountains Court. This is seen to be that of "a short female wearing a heavy velvet-like cloak who appears so normal that staff have been known to greet her."

A 1911 postcard from Hampton Court Palace with an illustration of one of their many apparitions.

BEATTIES

A model shop is not the sort of place one normally associates with phantoms, but here in Eden Street, according to both the *Kingston Borough News* and Barbara Russell, in 1980 the ghost of a woman dressed in "Saxon clothing surrounded by a mist" walked right through the shop, having been seen by the assistant manager, and her presence felt by other members of the staff.

Later, in 1999, two unusual figures were seen, one man wearing a cape, the other with a tall hat, but for such a fleeting moment that the witnesses could recall nothing more.

It seems that the site was formerly occupied by Hodgson's Brewery in what was then Heathen Street, believed to be "genuinely haunted" prior to the development of the area.

13 COMMONSIDE EAST

Formerly known as Rose Cottage, this smart but rather narrow building facing Three Kings Pond, according to author James Clark, has been affected by various noisy poltergeist incidents prior to 1920 but also has been haunted by a visible ghost during the same period.

Clark is to be congratulated for establishing the facts relating to the phenomenon and the intriguing history that surely must be associated with this 18th century building.

When Mrs. Burton lived in the cottage in the 1920s, as well as other witnesses, she saw the figure of "a stately middle-aged lady walk from the drawing room into the dining room, leaving behind a strong scent of lavender." The ghost for some unknown reason, became known as 'Lady Jane', but even when her perfumed visits ceased, the inexplicable movement of objects continued. Heavy footsteps were also heard several times, hurrying upstairs and, following the numbering of the house by the Council, "contents of cupboards were flung about by the unseen force" and even small items of furniture were thrown across the rooms.

Coincidentally though, when the number plate was removed from the front door, the physical phenomena ceased, though there might have been some connection with the discovery of an ancient well in the drawing room. The mysterious noises that had been heard "fairly frequently" stopped when the aged structure was filled in and sealed, and the visits of Lady Jane ceased, at least until 1977, when a building service company bought the house and converted it to office premises.

A member of the staff, Susan Maxwell, told James Clark that when she was working there in 1998, several weird incidents occurred, one being the overpowering smell of lavender being experienced, whilst others included documents and office equipment suddenly vanishing only to reappear months later in the most obvious places.

Rose Cottage, Mitcham.

Once, when Mrs Maxwell was alone in the building, she heard "an almighty crash", so loud she thought the wall had collapsed, but nothing was ever found to account for the sound. On another occasion, the front door refused to open and she had to call for assistance, only to find that her rescuers opened the door without any trouble, yet "it was as if there had been something strong and powerful behind it", she said. "Neither I nor my colleagues could even get the key in the lock and we had to wait for my sister to arrive. She simply opened it up with no trouble at all, but we never found any explanation for the problem. It was really weird but it never happened again."

The most memorable incident was when Susan was checking through the books one evening to see, quite suddenly, "my glass of water moving along the desk top. It stopped for a second, and then moved again for a couple of inches before finally reaching the end of the desk. I have always felt, though, that there was a presence within the cottage, but it was always quite friendly, though at times, a bit mischievous".

What Clark established in connection with the haunting was that in 1894 James Canham Read had been arrested in the house for the murder of one of his mistresses, Florrie Dennis. The murder weapon was never found but thought to have been thrown down the well that was discovered years later.

As to identifying the "mischievous character" involved, maybe she was the 'Lady Jane', seen though as a "middle-aged lady" back in the 1920s, or was it maybe the ghost of Florrie Dennis, thought to have been rather a 'tom-boy', even though she was a mother to a baby born in January 1894. Some even felt that another murder victim was deposited in the well of the demolished neighbouring property, numbered 15, but for the time being at least, the house, now a happy "and comfortable home" remains at peace.

SEVEN ISLANDS POND

In 1998 Tony Dow, a confirmed sceptic and member of the team of workers at a local distribution company, having finished his night shift at about three o'clock one morning, was taking a short cut home across Mitcham Common and walking past the series of gravel pits that over the years have filled with water and are now known as Seven Islands Pond, when he suddenly became aware of an unusual sound approaching him from behind.

The noise grew louder as it got nearer until he recognised it as that of a bicycle being ridden on grass. He turned round to see a young boy "about eight years old", on a white bicycle peddling furiously and looking intently at him, "staring directly into my eyes", Tony said. "That look was so intense and so fixed I was a bit unnerved, especially when the lad passed me, still staring, having turned round to continue looking at me over his shoulder. I didn't know how he could control the bike."

But then, as the pair drew near to the water's edge, Tony realised that all the sound had stopped and there was complete and utter silence. He also realised that the boy was clothed completely in white and by then the bike and the rider were actually on the water. With no sound from the wheels or any splash as the machine hit the pond, it "was so really weird that I just ran home", Tony admitted.

As a postscript that was published originally in the book *Strange Mitcham* by James Clark, the author admits that the original source was from two internet sites posted in May 1998, but since then all efforts to trace Mr. Dow have failed. Even an e-mail address given initially was found to be outdated. So, was the report a hoax, imagination or the re-enactment of a tragic accident years ago, which occurred in the depths of a hard winter, when the pond was frozen and the area was white with snow?

Seven Islands Pond, Mitcham.

Richmond

HAM HOUSE

This 17th century house was built by Sir Thomas Vavasaur, but the best known resident was the Countess of Dysart. It was she, Elizabeth Murray, whose first marriage ended with the death of her husband Sir Lionel Tollemache and who later married John Maitland, the Duke of Lauderdale.

A number of custodians and stewards have often reported hearing footsteps ascending the Great Stairway until reaching the second floor where they cease, though later are heard to descend, accompanied by "a trail of the perfume of roses." What is thought to be the ghost of Elizabeth has actually appeared in the Chapel, wearing a long black gown, having been mistaken on one occasion for a "dark statue", but she may also have been witnessed in the grounds. A figure of "a stout old lady" was seen by a visitor who enquired if "Queen Victoria was ever known to visit the house." Actually the Countess died in 1698 suffering from severe gout which, because of the difficulty in walking and the extreme pain, could well have considerably changed her appearance.

A far more recent death was when a 17 year-old, John Macfarlane, jumped from a window on the second floor because, it is believed, he was "a jilted lover" who had scratched his name on the sill of the window from which he threw himself. "A vague shape" has been seen on a number of occasions, near the window, accompanied by the sound of someone falling outside.

The South Lodge cottage is also affected by the sound of a tapping stick, believed to be that of the last Earl of Dysart, who owned the property until his death in 1935. He would call at the cottage every Christmas Eve to leave presents for the tenants.

RICHMOND PALACE

There is sadly little left of the original Royal Palace, rebuilt in 1498 by Henry VII, though the gateway remains a gentle and delightful reminder of the magnificent Tudor building that once graced the town until the 1650s when the main structure was demolished.

Part of the house and the Wardrobe building, on the left of the gateway, can however still be seen. It is in one of the windows overlooking the entrance and facing out towards the Green that "an image of a very old lady" has been seen, peering out "as if to recollect happier days." One witness told me that he thought that the "gentle phantom" had perhaps been hidden by the 18th century oriel window which was removed to restore the original appearance in 1939, for it was in far more recent times, starting in the late 1970s, that the infrequent sighting was first reported. "Someone has suggested it might be the ghost of Queen Victoria, but I somehow doubt that."

Richmond Palace gateway.

Ripley

THE TALBOT HOTEL

It was in July 2003 that I had the pleasure of speaking with Victoria Beecher, the general manager of this 15th century coaching inn. Its name originates from the extinct French hound that would run alongside the coaches on their way from London to the South Coast, whilst research indicates that this delightful 'watering hole' was one of those that proved to be highly popular during the raucous days of Henry VIII and his 'merry wives'.

Many famous historical personalities have stayed there, including Lady Hamilton whose former presence is said to be reminded by the legendary Lord Nelson's settle, his favourite seat when entertaining his "beautiful Emma".

For the 21st century traveller a private helicopter pad is available to the rear of the car park, though whether this is affected by the paranormal incidents is not known.

Talbot Hotel, Ripley.

In February 2003 a 'Paranormal Investigation Group' carried out an investigation into the phenomena that has been experienced here. Some of the members claimed to have felt "the presence of spirits" in rooms 6 and 7. In the former lights and the radio have often been found working though previously switched off by staff, and in room 9 "key holder problems have been experienced with doors and windows being found opened on their own."

Victoria Beecher's own experience is, I think, unique. A few weeks before our conversation she had made a telephonic reservation for a couple to stay in room 7 but on checking found a suitcase on the floor of the room and an unusual coat lying across the rumpled bed." Assuming that someone had forgotten to complete the daily records and that at least one guest was already in occupation she transferred the accommodation reservation to another room which was empty and ready to receive customers.

But only a couple of days later the incident was repeated, with a similar looking suitcase, coat and crumpled bed. Every member of the staff confirmed that the bed of room 7 appeared to have been slept in, though there was no record of anyone who had occupied the room. Only a short while later when about to remove the case and the coat both items were found to be missing and the bed ready made, "neat and tidy, waiting for the next guest."

A more tangible mystery has been the sighting, by a number of guests, of "a couple in old fashioned clothing" seen walking across the walled garden during summer evenings, before vanishing.

Sanderstead

SELSDON PARK

With an international reputation as established as the well known Selsdon Golf Course and it's associated hotel, publicity by way of a haunting is not really needed, yet this ancient 'mansion on the hill' continues to be the 'home' of an apparition of an unidentified 'lady in grey', witnessed a number of times in the Tudor corridor area.

The original building, probably a Saxon longhouse with wattle and daub walls and a thatched timber roof, was the family home of Aelfred the Earl of Surrey. His will of 891AD leaves the estate to his wife Werbur and his daughter Aelthryth, indicating the antiquity of the site.

In 1600 Harman Attwood purchased the estate and leased it to Christopher Bowyer who carried out extensive development work to form the core of the present structure.

The whole estate was sold in 1924 to Alan Sanderson who carried out more enlargements to create the longest hotel in England, an eighth of a mile, and the renowned golf course. The complex now encompasses facilities of an exclusive leisure club and beauty parlour offering 'vitality days and body treatment packages'.

The site of the appearance of the phantom lady however used to be, it is thought, the access to the servant's quarters at the end of a very narrow upright staircase and a group of smaller rooms. Some believe that the ghost is that of a servant girl, for the dress resembles that of a maid of the Edwardian or Victorian period, but from her stance the idea is that she is deeply upset, with her head bowed down and walking with the slow step of sorrow.

One of the most recent witnesses is Mrs. Williams, the executive head housekeeper, though others admit to have experienced phenomenon in the same area. "Lights going on and off" for no reason, and the sound of "quiet footsteps" having been heard. On another occasion in 2001 during a conference, one of the delegates reported seeing the figure "of a woman in a long grey dress walk silently across her room and then vanish on reaching the doorway." Thankfully though, nothing disturbs the tranquillity of the establishment.

FOX AND HOUNDS

This 'old' pub is not really that ancient, having been built as a hotel in the 1800s, but it seems that it has witnessed a number of incidents that have created some genuine hauntings.

According to Barbara and Tracy Russell, employees here have often heard some unseen person pacing along the corridor upstairs and Jason Peace, who moved in during the summer of 1992, has often listened to "ghostly footsteps padding up and down the stairs" on a number of occasions. He has also seen "a black shadow move through two closed doors and across the corridor in the hallway."

An overnight guest was astonished to see some golf clubs, packed inside a bag on the floor in the hall, suddenly "start to move about by themselves as though someone was searching for a special club." It was at the same time that she heard some "weird noises" coming from the empty kitchen, which was closed for the night, but when she went to investigate, all the four rings of the cooker were red hot and had obviously been on for some time, and yet the cooker was not switched on!

The cellars of the inn however seem to be the main epicentre of the activity, for it was here that a white-haired old man with a beard had been sighted on the stairs and a couple of managers who were playing music late at night, "suddenly felt a bit creepy" on hearing loud banging from the cellar, which failed to stop until they turned off the tape.

A similar case to the loud music incident was reported in the *Milwaukee Journal Sentinel* of November 17th 2002 in which a mother and her son in Ellicott City, north of Washington, were "terrorised by something" which seemed to be associated with the playing of loud music. One night when the boy was listening to a rather loud tape "things started to move around the room" and a psychic consultant was called in, who claimed that the trouble was caused by "the ghost of an old lady who didn't like the music." So as long as the volume was turned down, "the spectre said the scare tactics would cease." Sometimes "it is a pity that there are not more ghostly old ladies about", was one comment.

One parapsychologist summed up the problem, "it's all due to the vibes."

BINGO HALL, ROSE HILL

In what used to be the popular Gaumont Cinema, now an equally popular series of Bingo sessions attract visitors, but during the conversion three unfortunate deaths occurred. A boilerman fell to his death down a flight of stairs, one of the team of builders was killed in a tragic accident involving scaffolding and a night watchman was found dead one morning by the replacement security group.

When talking about the history of the place to a local writer one of the electricians involved in the conversion admitted to seeing the ghostly figure of a man standing at the top of one of the stairways, but on calling out to him saw the figure slowly vanish.

A number of reports from early morning cleaners, arriving at "about seven o'clock", have reported the appearance of "a man in grey standing in the Circle," but when approached "he just disappears." The manager of the club has also ascertained that local residents have heard the sounds of an organ playing in the early hours though, of course, the equipment was removed from the building many years ago.

Weybridge

BROOKLANDS RACE TRACK

This was once a well known international racing circuit built in 1907 at which enthusiasts, drivers and their supporters would congregate to see the famous, including the renowned Percy Lambert, and enjoy the thrills of the speeding vehicles, with experts competing for the honours, prizes and general achievement. It was here on February 15th 1913 that Lambert was killed whilst making a dramatic and thrilling attempt to capture the world speed record. He averaged over 110 mph for the first 120 laps but then a rear tyre burst on his Talbot and he was thrown off the track and killed.

Many claim that the ghost of Lambert has been seen since then, but recently other figures have been witnessed.

An executive of the museum staff assured me in May 2003 that what sounds like the description of a mechanic, though in "full

The air-raid shelter at Members Banking which stands on the spot where Percy Lambert was killed at Brooklands Motor Racing Circuit.

racing leathers" was clearly seen about nine years ago. "A couple of tourists from overseas were discussing the excitement of racing with one of the staff here and asked about the re-enactment, but were assured that there was no such function, nor any filming that could account for the mystery figure that they had seen walking on the part of the circuit known as the Members Banking."

This is not the only weird incident recorded on the site in recent times. "Lights of cars and commercial vehicles parked near the spot suddenly come on by themselves, and what is really peculiar, dogs taken on a walk in the area refuse point blank to go past the spot where Lambert was killed. They just sit down and refuse to move, and howl their heads off. It all happens at the back of the Members Hill."

The figure of the mechanic in white overalls and carrying a helmet has also been seen to walk across the car park and disappear whilst the witnesses watch. "A few months ago," I was told, "a team of contractors who were staying the night on the old track, unofficially, to enable them to catch up with some outstanding work, were all a little peeved, they said, at being kept awake at two in the morning by the sound of cars racing round the track - in the darkness. Rather a crazy and totally unreal situation."

GRANTLEY ARMS

Although the landlord, Mike Phair, has been here only for "about a year," he has heard so much about the two ghosts of the pub and the associated bakery from regular customers and local residents, that he has come to accept that this 17th century establishment is haunted.

He told me in April 2003 that "only a few weeks ago" a regular customer assured him that he had witnessed one of the spectral visitors "in the usual place, just about to walk up the stairs. He looks like a monk in a brownish habit, but he disappears before you can really get a good look at him." His visits usually occur at about Christmas time, but "no, it's not just to get into the spirit of the thing, but he does seem to dislike that time of the year. There is always a bit of 'a feeling', especially in that spot by the stairs."

The other figure, that of a young woman, is seen only "very occasionally and then only when there is a lady staying here."

The previous landlord confirmed that this ancient inn rests on the site of a mediaeval hostelry, administered by monks to provide food and accommodation for travellers and the many pilgrims on their way to Guildford and beyond. She also stated that she too had seen the ghostly monk and also knew of the spectral female who seems to dislike the arrival of any other woman overnight guest. "There is something about the Yuletide period that seems to provoke problems, such as the destruction of all our Christmas decorations on one occasion."

I am reminded of 'the leaking tomb of a Norman knight' in the nearby church which, up to the 1970s "nearly always emitted a brownish liquid from beneath its lid, always at Christmas time," but for which a rational explanation was later found, associated with the adjoining Cranleigh waters.

HIGH STREET

High Street, Wonersh.

Late in the 1960s a BEA pilot, living in the adjoining village of Bramley, near Guildford, was returning home in the evening, having collected his young daughter from her dancing lessons in Shalford, and was slowing up on approaching the High Street, having seen a couple of figures on the road, and as one was a large brown horse he did not want to frighten them. He commented on their appearance to his young passenger, but was astonished that instead of seeing the animal being led by "a rather tatty old gypsy woman", the girl could only see "a funny old lady with her arm in the air", and was worried that she was unable to observe the animal.

Both images, however, vanished on nearing the bridge over Cranleigh Waters, the tributary to the River Wey before it reached Guildford and the old Arun Canal.

Some ten years later a house in Linersh Wood Close, with its garden encompassing a portion of the stream, was sold to a family who confirmed finding remains of a stone-built bridge on the banks of the river, which had already been recorded as being from the mediaeval period by an expert from Surrey Archaeological Society. But also found on the stream bed were a couple of ancient horseshoes and some bones, later established to be those of a large horse.

During research in 2001 I was assured by a colleague in Guildford that the couple, the horse and the 'Romany' had been seen by another motorist the previous year, before disappearing where the original bridge once existed.

Probably completely unconnected with these incidents a Professor of Zoology, who used to have a studio in Wonersh High Street, told me that he was able to stay there for only a few months as the feeling in the evenings was "too oppressive for comfort. I really felt it was evil. It was getting diabolical and I was getting really suicidal. I just had to get out."

Battle

BATTLE ABBEY

The ruins of this Abbey, founded by William the Conqueror to atone for the bloodshed in 1066, have really become established as one of the most attractive tourist sites in the country. Owned now by English Heritage for some years, it provides a venue for an increasing number of re-enactments of various wars and conflicts, calling for groups of enthusiasts from all over the country to assemble on 'special event days', but none that affected Tuesday 30 April 2002.

This day was "cold, wet and blustery" according to Jill Sutcliffe, a New Zealand teacher from a well-known preparatory school in Kent, who was one of the supervisory staff dealing with a party of 45 young children on a popular school visit to the Abbey. It was about 11 o'clock and like the group they had seen most of the ruins

Battle Abbey with the mysterious silhouette of a hanging figure in the open gateway.

The undercroft at Battle Abbey.

but with two young charges, a couple of nine year-old boys, she was leaving the medieval Undercroft and glanced over at the battlefield in front of her, but turned back to check that there was no other child in the cellar, when she realised that approaching her "apparently in rather a hurry and seemingly rather irritated by something" was a grey-haired monk, wearing a white habit with a prominent red belt. "I was about to greet him," she told me, "but thought he was obviously too busy, so bent down to urge the boys on, and to go up the stairs beside the Abbey cloister, when one of the lads said, 'I wonder who that monk is? He seems to be in a hurry'." The trio continued walking back to the main entrance but wondering where the man had got to, for "he seemed to have vanished." On arriving at the shop Jill enquired as to the reason why the party had not been told about the re-enactment, "or the filming or whatever it was. I could hardly believe it when we were assured that there was no re-enactment, no filming and certainly no monk on site. The two lads couldn't believe it either, and felt it must have been a joke or something. But eventually we had to accept that what we had seen was just one of the ghosts of Battle."

The site of the latest 'haunting' was that where one of the senior custodians on closing up for the night had clearly heard a voice from behind a door in the Undercroft cry out "Let me out, let me out," but behind the door is solid soil. It was here also that I interviewed a Ministry of Works maintenance man who had been upset by the sudden and unexpected appearance of a monk squatting beside him when repairing an archway in the same part of the cellars some twenty years ago.

The original monks of the Abbey were Benedictines, whose habit was black, hence Blackfriars, but one, Robert de St. Martin, left to form the first Cistercian Abbey in nearby Salehurst in the 13th Century and it was this group that wore white or light fawn clothing.

A few years ago James Minahane of St. Leonards wrote a report detailing a visit he made in August, with his mother, who had wanted to know the reason for ignoring the two monks that had passed him during his walk in the tree-lined path adjoining the main wall. The reason for this, he had to assure his mother, was that he had seen no-one when in the 'Monks Walk' and wondered what his mother was talking about. He was told that there were two monks, seemingly arguing together, one in black, the other in a "light fawn habit" and were walking away from the Abbey itself and passed within inches of James. The figures had disappeared on reaching the end of the path. (See *'Haunted Sussex Today'*)

This latest incident, witnessed by three visitors, only adds to the mystery of the 'Monk in white'.

The haunted corner of the main upper level dormitory at Battle Abbey.

BATTLEWOOD NURSING HOME

Jenny Marney of Battle was for many years up to April 2000 one of the team of qualified carers at this large substantial property "which occupies a secluded lightly-wooded area" adjoining the original Battle Hospital which now forms a group of executive-type flats and apartments.

With its 21 bedrooms and 4 bathrooms, a lift and two staircases, this Nursing Home, once a home for nurses as well, was offered for sale in 2002 as an ideal site for an hotel, or even a replacement clinic for the community, but it was a series of unusual incidents during its previous existence that affected residents and some members of staff.

"The atmosphere was always strange", I was told, "never really scary, just peculiar." The staff of "about 15"nurses and carers had frequently been told of events for which no rational explanation could be found but they too often witnessed examples of "a paranormal nature".

Several times on opening the door of a linen cupboard on the ground floor, "a mysterious force would push us as if someone was trying to get past us in a hurry. The last time it occurred was about eleven in the morning, never at night." One of the staff, Maralyn Hicks, was actually pushed down the stairs, but thankfully was not hurt.

On another occasion, referred to by a resident, a weird moving black shape appeared on the ceiling of her room, but it had also been seen by members of the caring team, who described it as a "pulsating shape on the top stairway which seemed to mould itself around the walls. It really was uncanny."

An unusual case of 'dislocation' occurred with Audrey, (a pseudonym), witnessed by one of the nurses who on passing the residents' room glanced in to see the pensioner sitting quietly in her chair, but was told seconds later by Kevin, another of the carers, that he had just helped put the lady into her bed, for she was completely unable to get there by herself. It was the same patient who had suffered a mysterious bruising on her arm on being

Battlewood Nursing Home.

"thrown out of bed", perhaps by the same psychokinetic force which affected the nearby linen cupboard.

Sometimes doors were found to be jammed shut for no reason and lights would "come on and off by themselves", but one of the most mystifying incidents was that of the sighting of a woman in "a flowing gown seemingly to disappear through an old doorway beside a wardrobe." It was this visible 'haunting' that was a reminder of another unknown ghostly apparition, but of a man "in his 30s", seen walking down a corridor in the same part of the building. "He was wearing a black heavy winter coat, a really long one, but we never found out who he was. He appeared several times though."

A typical poltergeist incident involved "a vase flying off a dressing table, straight across the room and smashing against the opposite wall".

The building itself appears to be of the 1930 period, but it is probably much older and is thought to be associated with the old Victorian workhouse that later became a home for the mentally sick. However no-one can offer any suggestion as to the cause of the sound of laughing children heard on a number of occasions, when the affected area on the top floor was completely empty, or the group of youngsters clearly heard singing in the evenings, but in no specific locality, on the ground floor. One phantom youngster who "visited" Room 15, was seen wearing "a pork pie hat" of a period associated with the 1930s. On another occasion a resident described the spectral figure of a tall young man with black hair, whose unannounced entry seemed to have caused the emergency bell system to operate, despite the fact that no-one was in the region of it at the time.

The varied and numerous hauntings have, one assumes, now ceased as the 'change of use' has now been approved.

GEORGE HOTEL

Sue Smith and her partner Nigel took over the lease of this major hotel in April 2002 and have, ever since, experienced various types of "weird incidents." Mainly the problem is the sound of mysterious footsteps heard walking firmly up the heavily carpeted stairs when the building was empty. One Japanese tourist, on her first visit to this country, also heard the noise but was "just interested," not even apprehensive, and assured her hosts that "the ghost is certainly a friendly one."

Daren, the night manager, who occupies a flat at the top of the building, has only occasionally heard the unknown visitor, but was a "little upset" on waking up one evening to feel a "strong presence of someone in the room watching me - just studying me. I'm afraid I just went downstairs for a cup of tea or something, in rather a hurry."

Sarah, the housekeeper, told me on a recent visit that a large chair from Room 2 had been found on the landing, but Nigel confirms that the inexplicable movement of chairs occurred "fairly frequently, it's a bit of a nuisance really."

In an old brochure, recently discovered, it is claimed that there has been a tavern or hotel on the site for over 500 years and at one time the George was a London Coaching Inn, offering horses and stabling facilities. The original ostler's cottage, in the course of rebuilding as an exclusive restaurant, is where a young lad was accidentally burnt to death many years ago.

Other "nuisance incidents" in the hotel itself include the repeated "turning off and on of lights and the signs of someone

George Hotel, Battle.

having slept in one of the rooms overnight," despite new locks having been fitted to the bedroom door. "Pillows show depressions above where the head of the visitor has lain, and chairs found to have been moved around in locked rooms, and as for the linen cupboard, we always find it open, despite being locked every night." This is one of the six rooms which at one time formed the huge ballroom.

Sue has discovered a number of legends and reports about the building which may account for the "happenings." During the Civil War period, it housed a military court and there is a belief that even Cromwell was supposed to have stayed here.

Lucca Bendiggio, of the associated 'Simply Italian' restaurant on the ground floor, told me that "about 3 years ago the then owners of the hotel had arranged a night watch in the basement and in Room 6, as both areas were supposed to be haunted." The room was affected, it was claimed, by the sudden arrival of the ghost of a mysterious old woman but, "like the soldier in the basement," no one appeared during the vigil. The lady, apparently, had hung herself sometime during the last century, but no-one seemed to know in which room, leaving the identity of the stair walker, as well, unidentified.

TANGLEWOOD, Stoddarts Lane

Not far from Mouseland Wood is this charming old cottage, formerly home to a woodcutter and his family. With its recent extensions and modernisation, few would realise that up to a few years ago it was haunted by the figure of a "grandmotherly-type of little old lady" who the previous owners often witnessed moving slowly through the ground floor rooms of "the really old part" of the building.

The current owner, Mrs Merlin, assured me that although her son, in his early twenties, had been a little "off put" by the sudden appearance of the "old dear," whilst they were still in the course of renovating the place, "she really is, or was, a lovely old soul, full of comfortable, friendly, family warmth, but she hasn't been seen now for some time. But there is always a chance, I suppose, we rather miss her."

Brightling
ST. THOMAS A BECKET CHURCH

Well known locally for the pyramid shaped tomb of 'Mad Jack' Fuller, also known as 'Honest Jack', a controversial Georgian M.P. and philanthropist who, incidentally, was not buried "seated in his armchair wearing a top hat and tails, this parish church is a fascinating building in an amalgam of styles. There is no part though that is earlier than the 13th century, except perhaps the doorway in the south wall, which could well date from the 11th century.

On entering through the 18th century porch and the Norman doorway visitors are perhaps affected by the rather dark surroundings caused by the 1820 barrel organ which shades over the entrance, though intrigued by the 'devil's door' added in the 14th century, which faces them.

What has also puzzled some has been the inexplicable feeling of intense sadness in St. Nicholas Chapel, which some attribute to the

Brightling Church.

number of tombs of young children hidden behind the altar cloth on the wall. A couple of members of the congregation have, in recent years, been affected by sudden and invisible pressure of such strength that one was pushed so hard against a pew that her rib was broken, and another suffered severe bruising to his head. On both occasions there were few visitors to witness the disturbing episodes, but the mysterious atmosphere of the church affects more than just regulars.

A former vicar, in the 1970s, told me that he could stand the pressure no longer and was "leaving there and then", whilst some believe that what is accepted as a form of haunting is caused by "Jack expressing his anger at being buried facing the wrong way," whilst others feel that it is because the devil's door was not completely covered, for the top acts as a window, or even because of the cluster of ley lines that surround the area stop before reaching the foundations, leaving the church "isolated and vulnerable."

Brighton

THE DRUID'S HEAD

According to John Rackham in his really excellent collection of *Brighton Ghosts, Hove Hauntings* (2001), some 24,000 residents in that specific area may well have experienced a haunting - though such a figure may prove to be rather misleading. What is a 'haunting' anyway and how was the experience recorded?

At the time of the Domesday Book in 1086, Brighton had a population of a mere 400, paying an annual 'rent' or 'tribute' of 4000 herrings. Since then, like several Sussex coastal towns, it has seen many changes and developments and some horrific incidents, like the French raids in the 16th century, creating an atmosphere of constant excitement often associated with the thrill of illegal activities.

It was in 1510 that the Druid's Head was erected, firstly as a private house, and only in the 19th century did it gain a licence to serve beer. The name arose from the discovery of an ancient circle of standing stones, and probably incorrectly associated with the Druids, in the locality some time ago.

During refurbishment in the 1960s two tunnels were revealed, one of which is thought to have been used by smugglers, the other, more romantically, by the Prince Regent to enable him to carry out secret meetings with his lady friends.

The manager in 1993, Simon Woodhall, reported that when he was acting as relief manager, shortly before assuming full executive duties there, he had heard some weird knockings on the wall between the kitchen and the lounge. "I dashed into the kitchen," he said, "but the room was empty. It was a bit creepy." A year later another member of the staff, Cindy Winkle, noticed a woman in a red dress standing behind one of the customers that she was serving at the bar, and because the barman himself seemed unoccupied at the time, Cindy asked him if he would serve the lady. But as she pointed the woman out, the figure faded away. Who the 'lady in red' was has never been established.

Druid's Head Pub, Brighton.

A local rumour has it that a smuggler died in one of the tunnels and he continues to be heard "stumbling around" in a sealed-off portion of the cellars. Two other ghosts have also been associated with the pub and they are thought to be responsible for the typical poltergeist activity frequently suffered there. This results in bottles and glasses moving and sliding along the bar "all by themselves." One of the witnesses to the ghost of a tall and distinguished-looking man, seen in the 1970s, confirmed that his daughters had also experienced his "visits." Another former barmaid, Katey McElroy, said that after closing time the lights would "go off and on without anyone being near the switches. We had the circuits checked and replaced but it made no difference. It was always when the temperature went down. It became frightening."

With its past history of riots, murders, smuggling and at times, general mayhem, it is perhaps surprising that there are not more cases of genuine phantoms, and I would suggest that Brighton must be fairly close to the title of 'the most haunted town in the South East'.

PRESTON MANOR

This delightful and charming old Georgian house was originally built in 1250, but has been owned by Brighton council since 1933.

The former owners, Sir Charles and Lady Thomas-Stafford died the previous year and it was decided to retain the atmosphere with

Preston Manor, Brighton.

the original furniture and fittings in their original state. This enables visitors to recapture the environment of 'times gone by', but also, it seems, to offer the possibility of experiencing what John Rackham calls "the supernatural".

Certainly some inexplicable phenomenon has often occurred in the building and was first reliably reported in the 1900s, during which the ghost of an unidentified White Lady appeared "frequently, about every six weeks."

The initial recorded sighting was in 1896 when Lily MacDonald followed the apparition through the billiard room to the foot of the stairs where she tried to clasp the phantom only to realise that her arm had gone right through the figure which instantly vanished. On another occasion her sister Diana spotted the White Lady standing on the stairway and was about to ask who she was when the phantom faded in front of her.

A Captain Sandeman was another witness to the haunting and it was as a result of his encounter that a seance was arranged with a well-known, but rather unreliable medium, Mrs. Goodrich Freer. During the course of the proceedings it was stated that the White Lady was a nun named Caroline, but she was accompanied by another named Agnes, both from 1535. She, Caroline, claimed that a tunnel from the manor ran to the sea and "it could have been used if the enemies attacked the coast."

It is perhaps of relevance to mention that David Beevers, the curator at the time of my visit in the 1970s, told me that recent restoration work had revealed a bricked-up entrance to what sounded like a substantial tunnel, "but any suggested excavations would, of course, have to wait for full approval from the Council."

After the séance, in January 1897, workmen called in to clear a blocked drain uncovered the skeleton of a woman about 50 years of age, but from the condition of the bones the body was judged to be well over 300 years old. The remains were later buried in the nearby churchyard. But the haunting continued.

The ghostly figure of a woman dressed in a long black gown has been seen to walk through the open French windows into the garden where she disappears, and various examples of poltergeist phenomena have also been reported in the South West bedroom. Here the sound of strange tappings have been heard and, more especially, "a new silk dress hung in the cupboard was found to be riddled with small diamond shaped holes." It is not known whether this was the same cupboard, the emanations from which affected a Southern TV film crew's equipment which so frequently failed when directed at a corner cupboard, that the team were reluctantly forced to record another portion of the room. The four-poster bed there is also affected, it seems, by some paranormal influence.

In 1900 Mrs. Maguiac, (Diana MacDonald), had the impression of someone "immensely evil" leaning over her and sighing, which severely frightened her. Some time later a Mrs. Studd saw a man's hand gripping one of the bedposts before fading away.

Following an earlier report of mine relating to the weird atmosphere of that particular room, I was told that this could be due to "the shameful activities of Lady Stamford," but have been unable to find any details to confirm this rather vague comment.

It is of course doubtful that the Brighton Council will authorise excavations, which would prove costly, and of little benefit to the community, but with the interest in archaeology on the increase, one can never tell.

Haunted bedroom at Preston Manor.

THEATRE ROYAL

This well-known theatre in the heart of Brighton has long been known to house a ghostly grey lady, though she has never been positively identified. The building itself is formed from a collection of Victorian fisherman's cottages and a larger home, used to extend one of the upper floors.

An earlier witness to the phantom described her as a woman of about fifty years of age wearing a long grey full-skirted dress with a sort of grey veiling on her head, but as she reached the end of the corridor she just faded away. Some seem to accept that the ghost is that of Sarah Bernhardt, but provide no reason for her return.

A far more recent sighting was in February 2002 by the young son of one of the many theatregoers who wanted to know who the "tall lady in funny old clothes was". She appeared to him to be sitting on a 'prop box' at the side of the stage, actually during one of the performances. The boy's parents later admitted that they saw "something in a vague shape in the corner, by the box", but were unable to confirm that it was 'the grey lady' herself.

One aspect is fully agreed by everyone who has seen her. "She is a kindly soul" and "not at all scary".

Eastbourne

DEVONSHIRE PARK THEATRE

Opened in 1884, this popular entertainment centre, commissioned by the 7th Duke of Devonshire, saw the first season with *After the Wedding* as a successful launch which continued to flourish under the directorship of Stanton Triggs.

In 1903 a vast remodelling project was undertaken and then some 30 years ago, further modernisation was carried out to provide the staff room and refreshment preparation area.

The Eastbourne Corporation acquired the lease of the theatre in the late 1950s and in 1974 assumed management of it. Established as a real home for variety, audiences have been delighted by performances from such 'stars' as Harry Tait, George Formby and Diana Dors.

Following the close of *Aladdin* pantomime in January 2002, the Dress Circle was completely refurbished, which perhaps disturbed the atmosphere enough to cause a new haunting. There have been tales of ghostly happenings at the theatre for some years, but the most recent experience was that reported in

The auditorium of the Devonshire Park Theatre, Eastbourne.

the summer of 2002 by Stacey Barnes, a member of the Box Office staff.

"I heard a noise coming from the freshly-decorated toilets," she said "and went to investigate, but they were empty. But just as I was leaving all the taps started to run and the systems began flushing, but I don't think it was due to our 'resident' ghost though."

This 'resident' phantom has been witnessed in the orchestra pit over the years, and is seen as a violinist in white tie and tails and is thought to be the ghost of John Woodward, one of the musicians who died in the Titanic disaster in 1912.

But what is not so well known is the unidentified spectral woman who has been seen walking "one of the corridors to the left hand stalls." It seems that she has become so accepted that witnesses are expected to greet her with "Good evening Mam", to dispel her appearance. Occasionally trays of teacups have been found in disarray following her appearance, but who she is and why she haunts remains unknown.

Flimwell

COUNTRY FURNITURE BARN (Hare & Hounds), Hawkhurst Road

The Country Furniture Barn at Flimwell.

Once a popular old tavern at the crossroads of the main London to Hastings road and the east - west routes between Haywards Heath and Kent, the large 17th century building now houses a vast and varied collection of individually hand-made wooden furniture, not just from local experts but also from those overseas, such as Korea and Mexico. In 1765 a lease of 21 years for the coaching inn was granted to Thomas Hilder but in 1806 the tenant was Samuel Vidler who held the property for a rent of 7s 6d. Massive beds now juggle with unique rocking chairs for space, and exquisite tables nestle beside stools and desks in the former saloon bar.

Lynn Merlin, part-owner of the Emporium, told me, whilst admiring the extensive range of items in what was originally the stable block, that the family took over the site about four years ago, in 1998. It was a couple of years after this that her father-in-law heard someone walking upstairs that no longer existed. "It was necessary to remove that particular staircase in order to provide a wide selection and make it easier to move items around," she said, "but on looking over where the stairs had been, he saw the figure of a woman, in her thirties, I gather, with long dark hair and a long dark skirt. She was just standing on the upper floor. As she has now been seen more than once by visitors and friends we have come to call her 'Mary' but who she is or why she appears we have no idea." Her appearance is always in the morning on the first floor, where she walks from the site of the top of the stairs across the room before just fading away.

Another unknown ghost who inhabits the building is, surprisingly for an old pub, that of a young boy "of about six years old. He has been seen by Bill and a couple of customers standing behind one of the new beds we have by the front wall, only in the afternoons, about tea time."

Both figures are accepted as being of "kindly people" and as they disturb no-one are accepted as part of the comfortable, friendly atmosphere of the place.

Forest Row

BRAMBLETYE

An illustration of Brambletye House from The Mirror, 20th October 1827.

Just on the border of East and West Sussex and off the A22, Lewes Road, a lane leads to the ruins of Brambletye House or 'Castle' as it is known locally. It can also be reached by using the Forest Way, a former railway line that connects East Grinstead with Forest Row, and has been described as "the most interesting of the old East Grinstead Manors."

However, in 1827, the picturesque ruin was featured on the front cover of the small twopenny weekly magazine, *The Mirror*, published by J. Limbird of 143 The Strand, in which the fame of the building at the time was due to "Mr Smith's novel" of January 1826.

In the Domesday Book the house is named 'Branbertie', having been earlier owned by someone named Cola. He was not one of the Sussex Cokelers, though much later a Parliamentary Colonel Okey was involved with the owner, Lord Crompton, and "it was speedily taken when sad havoc was committed by the soldiery, with every symbol of rank and gentility being wantonly mutilated or destroyed." At the time of the Commonwealth Brambletye was the focus of many a Cavalier conspiracy but over the years deteriorated to become eventually a desolate and forlorn ruin.

It will be seen that the moated house was furnished with a ponderous drawbridge and, even then, in 1827, "it was consequently haunted."

In 1322 a Francis Aldham forfeited Brambletye to Pomcius de Controne , the King's Physician, and was later hanged for treason, though ownership reverted to the Aldham's family later. By 1411 John Pelham, of the Seyntclere family, had the manor of "Brambiltye £2 and the manor of Lavertye, worth nothing beyond reprises." In 1473 a jury found that Elizabeth, wife of Richard

A modern view of Brambletye.

Lewkenor, was the co-heiress of Sir William Bulleyn, but it was probably Lewkenor who actually built the original house which preceded the current remains. By 1579 the Pickas or Pykas family were in possession and in 1586 Drew Pickesse was returned as MP for East Grinstead. Then the Earl of Dorset held it for the king, but the next owner was Sir Henry Compton though the last known occupier of the mansion or castle, as it had become known, was Sir James Richards of a French family which had come over with Queen Henrietta Maria "the unfortunate wife of Charles I."

Just to confuse everybody, in 1774 Charles Biddulph was owner of the manor and his family continued to hold it until 1866. In 1903 the existing mansion was partially destroyed by fire but immediately rebuilt.

Recent lords of the manor and owners were Mr J. R. Peerless and Mr R. W. Peerless of East Grinstead, "copyhold being subject to heriot and fine - the beast payable to the lord on the decease of the tenant."

Simon Kerr, Information Officer of East Grinstead, confirmed to me that a number of people remain convinced that the ruin is "well and truly haunted" and few venture there at night because of the "shuddering feeling of dread," but details of the "mysterious figure seen near the Castle" remain unidentified.

Guestling

BUCKSWOOD SCHOOL

Formerly known as 'Broomham', this fascinating building which now houses an international boarding school accommodating some 120 pupils from as wide an ethnic horizon as Nigeria to Peru, is thought to have been built in the 15th century by Sir John de Stonelink. Ownership eventually passed by marriage to Richard, second son of the well known Ashburnham family and remained with them for over 500 years.

It was at one time home to the Bishop of Chichester, though by then the estate consisted of a working farm, or as a survey in 1810 described it, "an extensive stable and barns." In 1926 the original west front was demolished and extensive rebuilding resulted in the house as it stands today.

What has puzzled some visiting parents in recent years though, as well as staff members and naturally a few of the children, according to Ann Prince, Head Matron from 1985 to 1998, has been the appearance of a young boy, dressed in clothing of the 1920-30 period, "probably about seven years of age" who seemed to be searching for something special in one of the corridors leading to the scullery. One of the pupils was a little upset by seeing him and he called out "Go away, please," before the "vague figure" just faded away. The youngster is hardly ever seen these days, but now toys have been found to have been moved inexplicably, hidden or

An 18th century drawing of 'Broomham'.

Buckswood School, Guestling, formerly known as Broomham.

even "simply vanished," and sounds of "light footsteps along the corridor are heard." Some residents accept that the little lad is probably responsible for the "vanishing playthings."

More mystifying, though, is the appearance of a middle-aged woman in "what looks like a long black cloak and hood, rather similar to that of a monk's habit." seen walking along the same corridor that leads to the washroom. "Several of the children have seen and asked about her, especially as she disappears within seconds of her sudden arrival," but Margaret Taylor, wife of a former bailiff of the estate, assured me that "so far, no one has ever found either of the 'visitors' at all frightening. Why should they?"

Hastings

OLD BANK HOUSE

Only a few doors from the Town Hall Museum in the High Street, in the heart of the old town region of Hastings, this former bank now offers delightful and comfortable accommodation as a fully accredited guest house for tourists and visitors. It also provides an opportunity to witness what is thought to be one of the town's former residents.

The Old Bank House was originally built in 1425 as the home of a wool merchant, but in 1540 was re-constructed and again in 1700 altered to accommodate various requirements when the rear portion of the property was rebuilt.

In 1791 the original Hastings Old Bank was founded there by a group of businessmen including Messrs. Tilden, Hilder and Gill. Mr. Gill's son-in-law, William Scrivens, became a partner, as did his son George, who lived above the bank with his family. Their parlour has

Old Bank House, Hastings.

The corner of the hallway at Hastings Old Bank House, where a lady has been observed to hang up her cloak.

now become one of the bedrooms.

As with many such buildings in a busy and attractive seaside resort, the house continued to be altered and adapted to the requirements of the new owners and at one time was Ye Olde Shippe Tea Rooms. It is now owned by Richard Sumner, a former lecturer in history and politics who also provides scripts and programmes for the BBC Radio and TV, who was surprised to learn from one of his friends, Iris Turton, that she had witnessed a ghostly figure one evening, in the hallway. "It was of a lady in a high-waisted gown, and she was wearing a deep poke bonnet. She was taking off her cloak whilst moving towards the closet, passing right through a small coffee table, and appeared to be about to hang up the cloak on the door of the cupboard. But just as she reached it, she vanished."

Mrs. Turton was unable to see the face of the unknown visitor, because of the outlines of her bonnet, "but she had a sort of warm, kindly presence, no way was it threatening or frightening. Perhaps she was a former housekeeper."

Richard himself has never seen the phantom, though occasionally feels "something" when walking through the hall, and has learnt that there have been other witnesses to 'the woman in the bonnet'. The last occasion was in 1999 when again the appearance was "a pleasant occasion. I only hope to meet her myself someday," he said, "I like the idea of sharing my home with shades of the past."

Mountfield

ARCHERWOOD COTTAGE

Within the confines of Archer Wood, opposite the lane to the ancient Woodsdale Manor off the main road to Battle, this 'cottage', consists of a large country-style building recently extended from two smaller buildings.

In April 2002, Cilla Carey told me that the family moved in "some 17 years ago to enlarge the tiny woodland home, originally that of a forest worker, but since carrying out more recent developments and decorations, a number of "most unusual incidents" have occurred, involving not only herself, her husband Peter and her 10 year-old son, another Peter, but a number of guests and visitors since opening up the home as an overnight guest house for tourists.

Mainly, she told me, "bedding and the duvets move inexplicably in one specific bedroom and on one occasion a mattress in another room was seen to be spinning round by itself." In one fleeting

Archerwood Cottage, Mountfield.

incident, she saw the figure of what looked like a "ragamuffin girl, standing in the cellar, which has only recently been constructed. But it could well be on ancient foundations."

Cilla was told that a soldier died there in the 17th century and her husband has "been aware of a beggar-like character that seemed to push him in his back."

Peter junior has often referred to an elderly lady that he and his father have both seen and named "Nanny Cats". The whole family are cat lovers and own three delightful 'moggies'.

On a "really weird occasion", Cilla told me, "the whole family were in the garden and we suddenly realised that smoke was pouring out of the chimney although there was no fire in the grate, and when we rushed to find the cause, we found it was stone cold."

In the last few years a German TV film crew stayed for a couple of nights and they told of experiencing unusual sounds in one of the bedrooms and in the same room they have all felt an invisible cat walking over the bed at night. "It all seems rather peculiar", Cilla said, with a smile, "but it certainly doesn't frighten us."

CHURCH ROAD

The old mail-coach route to the ancient hamlet known as The Banks, from Taylor's Cottage through Bottonhold Wood, must have seen and experienced many varying incidents affecting lives and the atmosphere of aged by-ways.

One of these appears to remain as the sound of horse's hooves and the rumble of coach wheels, heard occasionally by locals in the area. A former community nurse, Ruby Willis, assured me one evening, some 15 years ago, she ran to the window of her cottage on hearing the noise and, being startled by it, wanted to see the cause, but "despite the clomping of the horses passing the house, there was nothing to be seen. It was weird."

However, on discussing the incident with a neighbour, David Walter, she learnt that he too had heard the sound of what was possibly a ghostly coach and horses on its way from visiting the 14th century Glottenham Manor on the outskirts of Robertsbridge. Others have also been mystified by the unseen transport.

VILLAGE HALL

Mountfield Village Hall

This central pivot for the local community was built by the Egerton family in memory of Mabelle, wife of Charles and daughter of Lord and Lady Brassey and opened in 1928. Sited within yards of the Parish church, it has been home for a considerable variety of events and activities, not all exclusively connected with the village. It was a NAAFI canteen and Home Guard drill hall during the war and has been used for exhibitions, pantos, as a dog training area, a dance hall, bingo hall and Polling Station; but it is mainly used today for public meetings, for the Parish Council and as the Mountfield Men's Clubroom, in fact anything that involves anyone associated with the locality to aid and assist the community generally in their activities, politically or simply for their enjoyment.

Some 12 years ago in the autumn, Colin Harmer, now chairman of the Parish Council, and a fellow committee member, Dennis

Smith, on preparing to 'open up' for the Men's Club one evening at about 7.30, realised that someone was already in the building despite it being locked. "We could hear them walking about the hall, yet it was in darkness". On entering, the couple clearly heard the footsteps moving towards the stage area, but as soon as the lights were switched on the noise ceased and the men realised that they were alone. Colin told me that "there always seems to be a bit of an atmosphere when approaching the left-hand side of the stage, near a portrait hanging on the wall. The eyes of the lady seem to follow you, but the footsteps were those of a man. We spent some time looking round the building trying to find an explanation, but had to accept that there was no-one else there and no signs of anyone having visited the place that day. If it wasn't for the fact that a number of people have commented on the coldness at that spot, and even a dog having been affected, I would have thought we might have imagined the whole incident. But at least it doesn't harm anyone, but we would like to know what it is that caused the footsteps and the coldness."

Pevensey

PEVENSEY CASTLE

This ancient ruin, a mix of Roman, Saxon and even 1940 construction, is of course highly suitable for a haunting - and it is.

Up to some years ago a tall female figure was seen gliding along the top of the outer walls, and was thought to be that of Lady Pelham, a supporter of Lord Bolingbroke who owned the building. Her appearance was officially recorded by the authorities at the time of her appearance, but no such phantom has been witnessed here "for decades".

What has puzzled not only the custodians, but a group of archaeologists who were working on an investigation of the chapel foundations in the centre of the ruins, were mysterious footprints seen in the dew-covered grass early in the mornings, on a couple of occasions, leading from the site to the outer wall, though none to the site. These prints were found to have been duplicated in a small snowstorm the following year, in 2003. Was the joker involved, who walked backwards on two occasions, just for a giggle? Maybe.

The atmosphere surrounding the entrance to the dungeon, near the entrance, remains however as one that severely affects dogs that refuse even to consider walking down the stairway to the punishment cell below.

The west side of Pevensey Castle.

Robertsbridge

BUSHEYGATE

Despite what one author claims, Busheygate is not an area but was originally a pair of farm workers' cottages initially known as number one and number two Cherry Tree Cottages. They were built in 1725 mainly from stones taken from the 13th century Glottenham 'Castle', a

Busheygate, Robertsbridge.

nearby moated manor house, the ruins of which could still be viewed in the 1970s.

The current owner assured me that like so many other people she finds the atmosphere of her home "absolutely delightful, but when I moved here in 1996, there was a bit of a puzzle. When alone in one of the bedrooms I would often hear the sound of people talking below the chimney breast as if at a party, but it was all a bit of a muddle. I couldn't distinguish any words and I only heard the sound in the evenings. But other people told me that they had heard voices as well."

A previous owner had experienced similar phenomena but in the kitchen of the other cottage. He thought the voices were of several young children "playing and squealing with happiness and excitement." Only a few days after he moved there he learnt that the cottage had for many years been the home for "at least three, sometimes as many as five, children. Their joy still pervades the place it seems."

One of the other puzzles, though, was the sighting in 1978 of a young girl of "about 18 years of age, looking over the hedge bordering the adjoining field." She had been seen "occasionally" by a number of former tenants, owners and visitors who described her wearing "a light coloured smock-like jacket. She just seems to be waiting for someone, perhaps her boyfriend." One witness was disappointed because she vanished after only about ten seconds, "like a puff of smoke. I reckon she was one of the milkmaids from the olden days." But she was a happy one, for she has always been seen to be smiling.

POPPINGHOLE LANE

According to Judith Glover, this twisting rather narrow country lane was the route to the Sussex community of Poppa, Poppa's Hoaeth or Home, the centre of which remains as Poppinghole Farm, a few yards from the unfortunately named Starven Wood.

One afternoon in the 1980s, Kerrie Micklejohn, then a bank teller but now a hospital car driver, was taking her two young nieces, of 8 and 10, back home after school, and on reaching the hill known locally as Jail Hill, between Walter's Farm and Poppinghole Farm, was a little surprised to see a woman in "full Victorian style riding habit, with a tall hat and seated side-saddle, on a beautiful chestnut horse, coming towards us." She glanced at her passengers commenting about the unusual looking rider, but on looking back at the road, saw it was empty. "Where has she gone to?", but the young girls were even more puzzled for neither had seen the woman nor the horse.

There is a record, it is believed, of a fatal accident at the site, when a hunt suffered from a series of inexplicable tragedies in the late Victorian era, which could well account for the mysterious figure.

Rye

MERMAID INN

This delightfully ancient but fully modernised hotel started life in the late 15th century as a hostelry in the coaching days, housing pack horses in the stables at the rear.

Mermaid Inn, Rye.

Like several places in Rye, though, it was also to become a notorious meeting place for smugglers, pirates and highwaymen, but by 1913 had become a highly reputable club, during which the owner reported seeing a "phantom duel between two Cavalier soldiers in one of the bedrooms. The fight continued out onto the landing where the couple vanished like a puff of smoke."

In the mid-17th century, there were some 40 ale houses and inn-keepers in Rye, all fighting for trade and custom, and some with Customs perhaps, but now as one of the Cinque Ports which remains of great importance on the South Coast life has become more tourist-oriented.

It was in 1994 that the Mermaid was used as a temporary base for the film and television crews making Stella Gibbons' *Cold Comfort Farm* but continues to be haunted by various unknown phantoms.

A bank manager and his wife, staying in room 10 in 1996, woke to find a man walking through the bathroom wall straight across the room until reaching the wall behind the bed, where he vanished. Room 18 has witnessed the figure of an old man more than once, sitting on the edge of the bed and room 5 is visited by the figure of "a dark-haired young woman".

There are, however, several other properties in the street affected by examples of the paranormal, two women in long gowns have been seen crossing the road near Jeakes House and the figure of a little boy wearing what looks like a kimono - perhaps it's a bathrobe - was often observed in a house on the corner of Watchbell Street.

UNION INN

This 15th century tavern, originally three cottages, was initially licensed in the 1420s and continues to attract customers, visitors, and more recently, ghost hunters for being one of the most genuinely haunted pubs in the county. Mention was made in an earlier book (*Haunted Sussex Today* 1997) of the ghost of a young golden-haired girl in a white dress that had been seen walking through the restaurant towards the kitchen, before vanishing. She appeared to be so solid that members of the staff have stood aside to let her pass, only to realise that she was "of a spectral nature" when she vanished in front of them.

A group of members of the long-established Ghost Club carried out an investigation in April 1990 and were, like most visitors, intrigued by the glass brick in the wall of the restaurant that is claimed to display bones of a still-born child. Doubts of this still remain, for despite a local coroner requesting burial of them, they are still to be seen, though are now undefinable. They were originally discovered about 35 years ago by a plumber fitting a new radiator in the room, but no-one is now really concerned about their situation, at least officially.

Union Inn, Rye.

In November 2002 and January 2003 groups from the Club returned again to establish whether the haunting had developed, or simply ceased as do so many cases when serious researchers arrive on the scene. Kathy Gearing, who organised the most recent overnight vigil,

The hole in the wall of the restaurant at the Union Inn where some bones have been found.

reported that the ghost still appears regularly. It is thought to be the daughter of a mortician, who rented the property, and she fell down the cellar steps and broke her neck. The year of the horrifying accident was put at 1856 by one of the 'sensitives' in the investigating team.

However, the girl is seen now to be "about 16-18 years of age and wearing a long red dress" and this has been confirmed by a couple of local witnesses in 2002. But Steve Dartnell, the landlord at the time of the visit, assured the Ghost Club members that he had seen another figure, "of a large man who walked through a closed bedroom door, go towards the window, turn and stride back again through the doorway." This has been described by other witnesses as the apparition of a seaman, dressed in dark blue jacket who has been haunting the upper floors for some time.

During the latest vigil by the Ghost Club members, several experienced inexplicable incidents in the same area. Three felt "something which produced a shiver down the spine" when sitting in the restaurant area; focussing of the camcorder proved impossible and two people, Shirley and Kathy, noticed a mysterious shadow when near the affected bedroom.

During the use of the electronic response detecting apparatus, a number of weird incidents occurred, including sudden temperature changes, feelings of being "touched and pinched", and one member of the group suffered an "audible slap on the head", from an invisible force. The gent's toilet also seems to be constantly affected by a 'hot spot' just above the cubicle wall, for "the needle of the Gaussmeter register went completely off the scale. The feeling in there, the gents, and in the kitchen was found by a couple to be more upsetting than anywhere else in the building."

Confirming the ever constant interest in the Union, the haunting and the investigations were featured in a series on the paranormal in one of 'UK Horizons' programmes on Satellite television in February 2003.

It was during my visit in 1994 that a colleague, an investigative journalist, became a little apprehensive when a door leading to the kitchen, a few feet from where we were sitting, suddenly and inexplicably opened and closed with a very loud 'bang' all by itself. It was only a few days earlier that I had revealed a previously hidden window in the original outer wall of the pub, which had been covered over when the restaurant was added to the structure as a lean-to many years ago.

Tangmere

TANGMERE AIRFIELD

During the last war Tangmere was one of the most strategic airfields in the region, sited only a few miles from Chichester and dominating the tiny village from which it gained its name. As with many such wartime centres it suffered from many bombings and some disastrous incidents.

One such experience was during the 1940s when a twin-engined Blenheim bomber crashed on the airfield, killing all four members of the American crew, and it is one of these airmen that is thought to have been seen as a ghost by Charles Golds, a local resident, when walking across the derelict runway with his four dogs one evening in April 2001.

However, the main haunted site is the old control tower, where not only uniformed figures have been seen, but vague whisperings and "conversations" from "invisible sources" experienced. There is also a museum on the site, reminding visitors of the wealth of activity that once affected the county, but which also contains a "phantom walker who occasionally moves some of the exhibits."

Upper Dicker

MICHELHAM PRIORY

Christopher Tuckett has been resident manager here for several years and is well aware of the stories regarding ghosts of this ancient Augustinian priory, including a lady in grey seen in the gatehouse near the entrance kiosk, and the occasional poltergeist 'visit' in which objects are moved by an invisible and mysterious force. One of the most recent incidents occurred in 1990 when another member of the staff saw a wig that had been temporarily placed on the back of a chair by one of the BBC film crew, during a sequence for a classic serial, "suddenly leap off and fly across the room".

Shortly after this, the manager went upstairs to check out the building before closing up for the night, when he noticed that the door to a small storeroom was half open. He glanced inside to see the window slowly opening by itself. "As far as I know," he told me, "that window had not been opened for decades. It had been rusted solid. Yet here it was moving silently all by itself. It was really weird. Thankfully I was able to close and fasten it properly, but only with some difficulty."

Michelham Priory.

To confirm that the popular attractive building really is haunted, late one night early in 2001 Christopher was completing his rounds before joining his wife in their flat on the upper floor, and glanced down over the stairwell to see someone walking along the corridor leading to the front door.

The photograph taken by Kathy Gearing in 2003 of a mysterious figure at Michelham Priory.

"I was astounded," he said. "I had checked the whole building and double checked all the doors were locked, and yet there was this figure strolling through as if they were a lunch time visitor. I was just about to run down to check them out when my wife called out asking about the sudden smell of lavender that had swept into the flat. It only lasted a few minutes and, of course, when I went down to try and find the unknown intruder I found absolutely nothing. I don't even know whether it was a man or a woman. I only saw the top of their head and what looked like a brown cloak or something. I wonder what will happen next?" What indeed?

In April 2003 an investigation group from the renowned Ghost Club visited the Priory and Kathy Gearing, the membership secretary of the Club, took a number of photos and illustrations via her camcorder, whilst in the building.

One of the pictures of the interior of the Prior's Chamber in which there is a full size model of a monk in his dark habit sitting in one corner, produced a startling effect, for there appears to be the image of a man facing the camera, whilst sitting down holding a light or some reflective item in each hand. What is also intriguing is that it seems to be casting a shadow on the wall beside the window, yet I have been assured by members of the team that there was no-one in front of the camera at the time Kathy was 'filming' and so far no-one has been able to offer any explanation for the mysterious figure, which to most observers looks like one of the modern day visitors, not some spectral creature of the past. The result is neither due to reflection nor a double exposure, though Kathy admits the flash operated after the shutter closed.

Wannock

FILCHING MANOR

Filching Manor.

In March 2003 I had the pleasure of speaking again to Paul Foulkes-Halbard about his fantastic collection of antiques, his veteran racing cars including the Bluebird K3 world record breaker, and the haunting experiences reported by friends, visitors and guests as well as members of his staff.

The Manor House itself, built in 1450, is truly a magnificent building full of warmth and charm with an aura of utter friendliness and now, a recent acquisition which was shown on television recently, a libation cup of solid brass, claimed by the British Museum to have been made in 710 AD. This, he believes, is in some way connected with Thomas Gilbert, later to be known as Thomas a Becket, "who fell in the millstream down the road in Wannock, but of the ghosts? - they are still around."

Mentioned in *Haunted Sussex Today* was the monk seen walking down the road which passes the entrance to the manor, in the afternoons, but also now the figure of a lady in a long dark semi-translucent dress walking silently in the grounds near the house. "Several people have seen her and all say she seems to be a friendly soul. The ghost of a servant girl has also been spotted, but what I can't understand is when in bed sometimes we hear a sort of 'plop, plopping' noise like the sound of someone in bare feet walking about, but of course there is never anyone there. Naturally we can't dismiss the idea of creaking floor boards especially in a house of this age, but it really is 'plop' not creak."

"We've heard the sound of the pail again, in the empty undercroft, together with a sort of muffled scream and murmuring as if a couple of people are whispering together. It's all a bit of a mystery, but no one is really bothered by it. It's just an aspect of life I suppose."

Whatlington

GATE FARM LODGE

This large and well-established residential home for elderly pensioners faces out towards Barrack Cottages and an area once well established as a camp site for troops both during WW I and WW II. On the other side of the village, more in Battle, an area known as Canadia acts as a permanent reminder of former tenants, temporarily housed there during the last war, some of whom carved their initials on walls of shops in Battle High Street and on the Abbey gateway.

Not only was Battle affected but some of the surrounding villages were 'commandeered' to house and accommodate not only troops massing for the 'second front' in the 1940s but earlier soldiers of the Napoleonic era. A large number of Italian and German prisoners of war were also temporarily housed in the region, but few reminders of those days remain.

It is from one specific lounge window in the front of this house that a number of residents claim to have seen " a group of soldiers doing their exercises" and on a couple of recent occasions, members of staff as well have witnessed a small group of "blokes in uniform" seemingly parading at the bottom of the driveway, before "simply vanishing as we watched."

Three of the witnesses, Molly, Katie and Dorothy were fascinated by the troops and reported the event to four members of the staff, but unfortunately, though the figures of the men have been clearly seen several times, they fail to remain long enough for the witnesses to recognise the period from which they originate. The strong belief is, though, that they are more likely to be World War I troops.

Winchelsea

GREYFRIARS

This ancient estate facing out over Friars Cliff has at its centre a large 19th century manor house, Greyfriars, once owned by the County Council as a residential home for the elderly. It was

18th Century engraving of Greyfriars, Winchelsea.

this building that was featured in a BBC TV dramatic, but somewhat distorted, reconstruction of the alleged murder in 1990 of Florence Jackson, one of the residents, by her aunt, Sheila Bowler, played in the film by Patricia Routledge. The feature, *Anybody's Nightmare*, like the documentary devoted to the same case in the 'Rough Justice' series, produced a lot of conflicting material, leaving the viewer more than a little mystified as to the genuine facts.

Regarding the structure itself, according to Arthur Mee, the well-known historian, "the fine house of Grey Friars has in it what is left of the 14th century monastery", which at one time had been a farmhouse and a chapel. A ruined chapel still stands only a few yards away from the main building and this, which belonged to the Friars Minors, established in 1224, is detailed in W.D. Cooper's book *'Winchelsea'*, which he published in 1850.

In 1819 Richard Stileman, the then owner of the estate, demolished the original mansion and erected the current house and in 1908 this was auctioned and a Mr and Mrs Freeman moved in, but it was obvious to the locals that it was the lady "who wore the trousers. She was very grand," wrote Margaret Muggeridge, and was never forgotten, though she died in 1928, her husband six years later and their son, Anthony, in 1971.

Diana Holman-Hunt tells of "true stories in essence, but not in

Greyfriars in 1784.

detail, of the old monk, a ghost alleged to haunt the Friars and the marsh," but it is not he that has been witnessed in recent times.

Until her death in 1998, the estate had been managed by a Mrs Anne Croggon, "a kindly soul, full of natural warmth, but with very strong character at times." It was during her administration that Greyfriars, owned by the Council from 1949, was sold in 1995 to become a privately run estate again, providing a happy home for a local family.

It was prior to this, though, that the ghost of a "tall woman in flamboyant white clothing" had been seen on a number of occasions by the night staff, and occasionally a resident, walking purposefully along a corridor leading to a new kitchen and flat. This 'new' sector was constructed some 20 years ago so the phantom certainly cannot be that of Mrs Croggan, who was "rather short and a little plump". It is this apparition that has also been seen during summer evenings standing in the nearby chapel ruins as if "enjoying the ambience, the charm and the atmosphere, before she fades away."

The identity of the "friendly lady in white" remains as mysterious as that of the young baby heard crying pitifully on a number of occasions and reported to Mrs Nye, matron of the Council home for 17 years. She told me that the cries were heard in Room 5 and its associated bathroom, that had at one time been the nursery, which is where a young boy died many years ago. "A pleasant but intriguing presence had been felt in Room 2 and very strongly in Room 1 in the new wing, but the haunting, if you can call it that, was more in the form of a sudden warm wind. Most peculiar, but not at all frightening."

Greyfriars now remains as a historic family estate housing a number of fascinating and haunting memories.

Picture Credits

Grateful thanks and acknowledgement is given to the following for reproduction of the illustrations in this work:

Front Cover	Author's collection
Pillared Room, 10 Downing Street	Author's illustration
Cobham Manor Riding Centre	Kent Messenger Group
Higham Park, Bridge	Patricia Gibb
Canterbury Cathedral	Author's collection
Dover Castle	Author's collection
Lion Hotel, Farningham	Trish Jones
Martello Tower No. 3, Folkestone	Shepway District Council
Groombridge Place	Chris Parker
Saltwood Castle	Author's collection
Otford Antiques & Collectors' Centre	Trish Jones
Pillow Talk, Margate	Author's collection
Old Oak Cottage, Minster	John Walford
Ye Olde Leather Bottel, Northfleet	Trish Jones
George Inn, Chertsey	Author's collection
Pizza Piazza, Farnham	Jean Parratt
Angel Hotel, Guildford	Author's collection
Illustration of Angel Hotel's ghost	Surrey Advertiser
Cloth Hall, Guildford	Philip Hutchinson
Guildford Castle	Philip Hutchinson
Guildford Museum	Philip Hutchinson
122 High Street, Guildford	Philip Hutchinson
Hampton Court Palace ghost	Author's collection
Rose Cottage, Mitcham	James Clark
Seven Islands Pond, Mitcham	James Clark
Richmond Palace Gateway	Author's collection
Talbot Hotel, Ripley	Author's collection
Members Banking, Brooklands	Brooklands Museum
High Street, Wonersh	Author's collection
Battle Abbey, gateway	Wendy Foran
Battle Abbey, undercroft	Daryl Burchmore
Battle Abbey, dormitory	Tom Perrott
Battlewood Nursing Home	Author's collection
George Hotel, Battle	Trish Jones
Brightling Church	Trish Jones
Druid's Head, Brighton	Author's collection
Preston Manor, Brighton	Author's collection
Devonshire Park Theatre, Eastbourne	G. Ivan Barnett
Country Furniture Barn, Flimwell	John Dawes
Brambletye, 1827 illustration	Author's collection
Brambletye photograph	Simon Kerr
Broomham, 18th Century illustration	Author's collection

Buckswood School, Guestling	Nicholas Taylor
Hastings Old Bank	Trish Jones
Archerwood Cottage, Mountfield	Trish Jones
Mountfield Village Hall	Trish Jones
Pevensey Castle	Author's collection
Busheygate, Robertsbridge	Author's collection
Mermaid Inn, Rye	Trish Jones
Union Inn, Rye	Tom Perrott
Michelham Priory	Author's collection
'Mysterious figure' at Michelham Priory	Kathy Geary
Filching Manor	Paul Foulkes-Halbard
Greyfriars, Winchelsea	Author's collection
Author photograph	Philip Carr

Bibliography

A History of Groombridge Place	by Barbara Maidment
A History of East Grinstead	by Michael Leppard
A Tapestry of Battle	by Battle Writers' Group
Brighton Ghosts, Hove Hauntings	by John Rackham
Ghostly Encounters	by Astrid St. Aubyn and Zahra Hanbury
Haunted Churches	by Graham McEwan
Haunted England	by Christina Hole
Haunted Farnham	by Jean Parsatt
Haunted Kent Today	by Andrew Green
Haunted Sussex Today	by Andrew Green
History of East Grinstead	by Wallace Henry Hills
History of Hastings Castle	by Charles Dawson
In Search of Ghosts	by Ian Wilson
Investigating the Paranormal	by Tony Cornell
Kings England - Sussex	by Arthur Mee
Mediaeval Ghost Stories	by Andrew Joynes
My Grandmothers and I	by Diana Holman-Hunt
Mysterious Kingston	by Barbara and Tracy Russell
Rooms of Mystery and Romance	by Allan Fey
Strange Kingston	by Barbara and Tracy Russell
Strange Mitcham	by James Clark
Surrey Ghosts Old and New	by Frances Stewart
Winchelsea	by W. D. Cooper
Winchelsea - a Port of Stranded Pride	by Malcolm Pratt

Newspapers and Magazines: Evening Argus (Brighton), The Mirror, The Daily Mail.

About the Author

ANDREW GREEN, BSc, MPhil, FETC was a member of the Society for Psychical Research from 1972, having written a number of books and several hundred articles on ghosts and hauntings, edited works on phenomena, appeared in numerous television and radio programmes on the paranormal, he was also appointed as a consultant to the Ghost Club. His activities have been featured nationally and internationally. A Sunday Times article dubbed him the 'Spectre Inspector'. In 1996 he was commissioned to examine alleged phenomena in the Royal Albert Hall, which was broadcast as updates on the news during his overnight investigations there and resulted in his inclusion in the BBC's Review of the Year.

Andrew's attraction to the paranormal began in 1944 when he took a photograph of an empty house where, between 1883 and 1934 twenty suicides and a murder had taken place. The print of this picture showed a young girl sitting at one of the upstairs windows, who had not been there when the picture was taken.

Andrew tutored adult courses in the south-east for over twenty-five years and lectured on hauntings. He had, however, no belief in life after death and believed that ghosts were a form of electro-magnetic energy usually created by someone living as a form of unconscious telepathy.

This is Andrew's seventeenth book and sadly his last. After suffering for many years from emphysema, a disease that increasingly debilitated and disabled him, he found it more and more difficult to write. Andrew passed away in May 2004. This manuscript was largely complete at the time of his death and has been prepared for publication from his papers by his friend and neighbour, Trish Jones.